KEEP CALM
AND
TRUST
GOD

DEVOTIONAL

JAKE AND KEITH PROVANCE

WORD & SPIRIT
PUBLISHING

Keep Calm and Trust God — Devotional
ISBN: 978-1-685730-54-3
Copyright © 2024 by Jake and Keith Provance
Published by Word and Spirit Publishing
P.O. Box 701403
Tulsa, Oklahoma 74170
wordandspiritpublishing.com

Creative concept by Ryan Provance

Dear Reader,

We are incredibly excited to introduce you to our latest book: a devotional that combines the encouragement and inspiration from our three best-selling books, *Keep Calm and Trust God, Volumes 1* and *2* and *Let Not Your Heart Be Troubled*. It is our sincere desire to provide you with a unique and powerful resource that will help you maintain your calm and trust in God throughout your daily life. At the time of this writing, *Keep Calm and Trust God* books have been immensely popular, reaching over one million copies sold, and we've received countless messages from readers just like you, who have found encouragement and strength within the pages of these volumes.

With this in mind, we have decided to transform these three volumes into a single, cohesive devotional that will guide you through each day of the month. This new devotional will retain all the cherished content you've come to love from the original volumes, but it will also include fresh quotes, Scriptures, narratives, and prayers to enrich your spiritual journey even further. We have expanded the chapters to thirty-one, allowing you to engage with a daily devotional every day of the month.

We also want to make this devotional a truly interactive and personalized experience for you. With that in mind, we've included a special feature: an additional page after each day's entry. This space is yours to capture your thoughts, feelings, and reflections as you engage with the devotional. Consider it your canvas to freely express your heart's desires, concerns, or revelations, turning this devotional into a cherished keepsake that reflects your unique spiritual journey. By combining the power of devotionals with the introspective nature of journaling, we hope to create a transformative experience that allows you to connect with God on an even deeper level.

At its core, this devotional is all about helping you maintain inner peace and unwavering faith in the midst of life's challenges. We know that when you trust in God, it becomes easier to navigate the uncertainties of life with a calm heart and a clear mind. Throughout this devotional, we hope to inspire and encourage you to face each day with renewed faith, knowing that God is always by your side. Our prayer for you is that this devotional will become a cherished companion in your walk with God, that it will help you grow in faith and deepen your relationship with Him. We look forward to joining you on this journey toward calmness and a greater trust in the Almighty. May this devotional bring you peace, hope, and a renewed sense of trust in God's unwavering love and guidance.

With warmest regards and blessings,

Jake and *Keith*

Table of Contents

Introduction

The British government coined the slogan "Keep Calm and Carry On" in 1939 as the threat of World War II loomed. In the event that Hitler's army invaded England, with the slogan posters were to be distributed to England's general population in an effort to galvanize their resolve to resist German aggression. Should Germany invade across the English Channel, it would be one of the darkest times in England's history.

Under the shadow of Nazi air raids and bombing runs, death and destruction, and a world thrown into chaos, the British government knew the people would need encouragement. The future of the free world teetered in the balance. And in those dark times, believers everywhere prayed fervently.

Thankfully, most of us will never have to face that kind of tragedy and adversity in our own lives. Nevertheless, today we find ourselves embroiled in a different kind of war.

Our lives seem to be under constant assault. Worry, fear, and anxiety threaten our peace of mind on a daily basis. Our society has accepted depression and discouragement as common social ailments. The pressures and stress of the daily grind robs us of the joy and peace God has intended for us to enjoy.

So where do we turn in these trying times? The same place the Christians in World War II did to God and His Word.

Just as with the British facing the threat of German invasion, we must "Keep Calm and Carry On." When adversity comes, however, simply keeping calm is not enough. We cannot fight the enemy of our soul with a slogan. Nor can we "carry on" in our own strength. We need to rely on and gain our strength from God. We need to trust Him completely and totally.

Whether we realize it or not, many of the battles we face in our lives today are spiritual battles, and we cannot win with just our own willpower. When trouble comes your way or when bad news hits you right between the eyes, be determined to replace fear with confidence in God, to replace worry with faith in Him, and to replace anxiety with His peace. Keep calm, and most of all, trust God.

God has promised to never leave you or forsake you. He wants to be a part of your life. When you need His help, all you have to do is ask. In your hour of greatest need, He will uphold you and sustain you. He will give you peace in the midst of the storms of life.

As you engage with this devotional, may you find comfort in the knowledge that God is on your side. He is with you and for you. He will never leave or abandon you. By His Spirit and through His Word you can overcome anything this world throws at you. We believe that the wisdom, scriptures, and prayers within these pages will help you build a deeper connection with God, enabling you to grow in your faith and experience His transformative power. Our prayer is that, as you read these pages you will find a renewed sense of purpose, joy, and peace in the loving embrace of our Heavenly Father. Together, let's face life's challenges with unwavering faith, knowing that God's love and guidance will carry us through even the darkest of times.

"The beginning of anxiety is the end of faith, and the beginning of true faith is the end of anxiety."

—George Mueller

We shall steer safely through every storm, so long as our heart is right, our intention fervent, our courage steadfast, and our trust fixed on God. If at times we are somewhat stunned by the tempest, never fear, Let us take breath, and go on afresh.

—Francis de Sales

1

Anxiety

Anxiety seems to be all around us, all the time. Sometimes, just the normal hassles of daily living can cause us to be anxious. Anxiety can steal our ability to enjoy friends, family, and life in general. Anxiety can contribute to high blood pressure, stomach or intestinal disorders, and heart attacks. It can even lead to panic attacks or nervous breakdowns.

Sure, life is full of challenges, conflicts, and stressful situations, but we don't have to let them produce anxiety in our lives. Whatever the cause or source, anxiety serves no good purpose. Life is too short to allow anxiety to steal the joy of living a peaceful, productive, and fulfilled life!

God provides the key to combating anxiety in Philippians 4:6-7: "Do not be anxious about anything, but in every situation, by prayer and petition, with thanksgiving, present your requests to God. And the peace of God, which transcends all understanding, will guard your hearts and your minds in Christ Jesus" (NIV).

That pretty much sums it up—prayer with thanksgiving produces peace. And not just any peace, but a supernatural peace that comes from God and that surpasses all human understanding! Isn't that good news?

Jesus said in John 14:27, "Stop allowing yourself to be anxious and disturbed: and do not permit yourself to be fearful and intimidated and cowardly and unsettled" (AMP). Based on that, Jesus must be telling us that living an anxiety-free life is a *choice*.

You can choose to rise above anxiety. Put your trust in God and refuse to be discouraged and agitated. Count your blessings! Put your confidence in Him, for He loves you, cares for you, and believes in you.

Acknowledging that we permit anxiety in our lives through what we choose to think on is the first step too breaking free of it. When we allow ourselves to focus on the wrong things, we are making an unconscious choice that opens the door for anxiety in our lives. We must recognize the active role we play in managing our thoughts and emotions and choosing to keep them fixed on the bible and on Christ. Even when anxious thoughts come, and they will, we choose to not permit them to intimidate us into inaction and instead choose to ground our thoughts on the Word of God. It's our response to these moments that determines victory or defeat. Will you sit and marinate in your anxiety and worried thoughts, or will you cast those anxious thoughts on the Lord and trust in Him.

The bible tells us to "stop allowing yourselves to be anxious" in John and in Philippians it tells us "Do not be anxious about anything." This means Anxiety is never good in your life. In any area that you have been battling anxiety in your life, there is a truth in God's Word, that if you will read it and believe it, then it will shatter anxiety's hold in your life in that area. Believe it, and fight off anxiety in your life. Shift your perspective onto what God has said, and begin experiencing life's moments fully, without the shadow of anxiety looming over you.

Prayer

Lord, Your Word says not to fret or have any anxiety about anything. You also said that when anxiety is present, I should cast those anxieties on You because you care for me. You said that in every circumstance and in everything, by prayer and with thanksgiving, I should continue to make my needs known to You, and when I do that, Your peace, which transcends all understanding, shall garrison and mount a guard over my heart and mind in Christ Jesus.

So, Lord, I take the time to do that now. Thank You for caring about me. Thank You for not leaving me helpless against the machinations of this world. Rather, You have provided me with faith and truth to use as a shield, which enables me to walk boldly in life. Father, I ask for Your help. Calm my anxious heart. I know that whatever I am facing, You are right there with me, for You have promised never to leave me nor forsake me. Help me to trust You despite the circumstances that surround me.

Lord, when I am tempted to be anxious, help me to speak Your promises, to overcome the attacks on my mind with answers from Your Word. Let me be quick to respond to any wrong thoughts or desires by replacing them with good thoughts. Thank You, Lord, that You light the way before me. You give me clear instructions, and You keep me firmly on the paths of righteousness. I put my complete trust in You. You are my shield and my refuge. You are my rock and my fortress. You are my hiding place and my strong tower. In the midst of the storm, You enlighten me with Your understanding, and You give me Your peace. I refuse to be anxious about anything.

In Jesus' name I pray, amen.

Scriptures

Humble yourselves, therefore, under God's mighty hand, that he may lift you up in due time. Cast all your anxiety on him because he cares for you. Be self-controlled and alert. Your enemy the devil prowls around like a roaring lion looking for someone to devour.

— 1 Peter 5:6-8 (NIV)

Do not fret *or* have any anxiety about anything, but in every circumstance *and* in everything, by prayer and petition (definite requests), with thanksgiving, continue to make your wants known to God. And God's peace [shall be yours, that tranquil state of a soul assured of its salvation through Christ, and so fearing nothing from God and being content with its earthly lot of whatever sort that is, that peace] which transcends all under-standing shall garrison *and* mount guard over your hearts and minds in Christ Jesus.

— Philippians 4:6-7 (AMP)

Anxiety weighs down the heart, but a kind word cheers it up."

— Proverbs 12:25 (NIV)

Who will rise up for me against the evildoers? Who will stand up for me against the workers of iniquity? Unless the Lord had been my help, My soul would soon have settled in silence. If I say, "My foot slips," Your mercy, O Lord, will hold me up. In the multitude of my anxieties within me, Your comforts delight my soul.

— Psalm 94:16-19 (NKJV)

Thoughts

"Anxiety is the natural result when our hopes are centered in anything short of God and His will for us."

—BILLY GRAHAM

"Worry implies that we don't quite trust God is big enough, powerful enough, or loving enough to take care of what's happening in our lives."

—Francis Chan

"Worry does not empty tomorrow of its sorrow, it empties today of its strength."

—Corrie Ten Boom
(Holocaust survivor)

2

Worry

We all face the daily opportunity to worry about something—our health, finances, family, jobs, the economy. The list is endless. If we let them, our worries can consume our lives!

Yet worry is so unproductive, it accomplishes nothing except producing anxiety, stress, and fear. Worry will rob you of your joy, peace, and faith. It can cloud your mind and often leads to irrational thinking.

You've never cured a loved one in the hospital by worrying about them. You've never paid a bill by worrying about how you are going to pay it. You have never solved a problem by worrying about it. You've never mended a broken relationship by worrying about it. Yet with the same amount of time, and effort that it took you to worry, you could have been praying which invites God to do what you can't these situations. Often, we confuse worrying with caring. Caring looks like praying for your loved one, visiting them, checking on their family, making them a meal etc. Worrying is just chronic fear masquerading as heartfelt concern. Worrying is your enemy, and it is robbing you from making a difference when others need you the most.

Worry's strength and hold on your life only grows if you dwell on your problems. But there is great news—God's plan is for you to live a worry-free life! You may be wondering, *How is that possible?* Simple: by putting your complete trust and confidence in God and His Word. God promised that He would never leave you or forsake you, and the Bible tells us in Matthew 6:25 not to worry about your life.

If you were to look through the eyes of your Heavenly Father, you would see that no situation or circumstance is too great for God! Our problems are actually quite small compared to how big our God is!

The secret so many people miss is that it's not enough to tell yourself not to worry about something; you have to *replace* worried thoughts with God's thoughts. When you dwell on the Word, you dwell on His thoughts. Paul refers to this process as "renewing your mind" in Romans 12:2. Making it a part of your daily routine to read, meditate, and speak God's Word will transform your life!

In this you become prepared In the relentless battle against worry, by embracing a mindset of gratitude and trust rooted in the truth of God's word. When worry starts to encroach upon your peace, shift your focus to the countless blessings in your life. Remember the times when you faced challenges, yet emerged stronger because of your faith. This deliberate act of gratitude helps to weaken the grip of worry, replacing it with a sense of hope and reassurance. As you cultivate this habit, you begin to see life through a lens of faith rather than fear, assured that God's guidance is constant, even in the midst of turmoil. This doesn't mean that challenges won't arise, but rather that your approach to them is one of calmness and confidence, rooted in the unwavering belief that with God, you are more than capable of overcoming any obstacle. This transformation in perspective is not just a temporary relief but a profound change that paves the way for a life filled with peace, purpose, and joy, unshaken by the ebb and flow of worldly concerns.

Prayer

Lord, thank You for Your deep love for me. Thank You that not a single day goes by that You aren't aware of my thoughts and the desires of my heart. Father, I know that worry serves no good purpose, and so I'm asking for Your help. Help me not to worry, but to instead fill my mind and my mouth with prayer and praise. Your Word says not to worry about food, drink, clothing—or even tomorrow. You've instructed me to seek You and Your reign in my life today. When I do that, then everything I was worried about in the first place will be taken care of, for my sake.

So, Father, I don't just ask for Your help not to worry, but I ask for Your help in seeking You each and every day. Set a watch at the door of my heart, keeping out anything that would cause me to worry. I ask that You would remind me of all that You have said in Your Word that combats the worry in my mind. I am looking to You to see me through every day of my life. In obedience to Your Word, I cast all my care, concern, and worry on You. Grant me Your peace to remain steady and calm in the midst of trouble. Help me to let Your peace rule and reign in my heart. I put my trust and confidence in You. I know You love me and care for me as a loving Father. I know You will not let me down. I believe that You are working everything out for my good.

Lord, reveal to me Your perfect will in this situation. Help me to keep looking to You and not let my heart be troubled or fearful. Help me to be spiritually strong and courageous and not let my emotions or feelings dictate my actions.

In Jesus' name, amen.

Scriptures

Therefore I tell you, do not worry about your life, what you will eat or drink; or about your body, what you will wear. Is not life more than food, and the body more than clothes? Look at the birds of the air; they do not sow or reap or store away in barns, and yet your heavenly Father feeds them. Are you not much more valuable than they? Can any one of you by worrying add a single hour to your life? "And why do you worry about clothes? See how the flowers of the field grow. They do not labor or spin. Yet I tell you that not even Solomon in all his splendor was dressed like one of these. If that is how God clothes the grass of the field, which is here today and tomorrow is thrown into the fire, will he not much more clothe you—you of little faith? So do not worry, saying, 'What shall we eat?' or 'What shall we drink?' or 'What shall we wear?' For the pagans run after all these things, and your heavenly Father knows that you need them. But seek first his kingdom and his righteousness, and all these things will be given to you as well. Therefore do not worry about tomorrow, for tomorrow will worry about itself. Each day has enough trouble of its own.

—MATTHEW 6:25-34 (NIV)

Cast thy burden upon the LORD, and he shall sustain thee: he shall never suffer the righteous to be moved.

—PSALM 55:22

What shall we then say to these things? If God be for us, who can be against us?

—ROMANS 8:31

Thoughts

....

....

....

....

....

....

....

....

....

....

....

....

....

....

....

....

....

....

....

....

....

....

....

....

....

"Worry is like a rocking chair: it gives you something to do but never gets you anywhere."

—ERMA BOMBECK

"I learned that courage was not the absence of fear, but the triumph over it. The brave man is not he who does not feel afraid, but he who conquers that fear."

—Nelson Mandela

The Arena

"It is not the critic who counts; not the man who points out how the strong man stumbles, or where the doer of deeds could have done them better. The credit belongs to the man who is actually in the arena, whose face is marred by dust and sweat and blood; who strives valiantly; who errs, who comes short again and again, because there is no effort without error and shortcoming; but who does actually strive to do the deeds; who knows great enthusiasms, the great devotions; who spends himself in a worthy cause; who at the best knows in the end the triumph of high achievement, and who at the worst, if he fails, at least fails while daring greatly, so that his place shall never be with those cold and timid souls who neither know victory nor defeat."

—Theodore Roosevelt

3

Fear

Fear is one of your Greatest Enemies. It can steal your joy, rob your peace, and paralyze your faith. It can dull your senses, confuse your mind, and produce irrational thoughts and behavior. Fear can cause us to say and do things we would never even consider under normal circumstances.

Fear takes on many forms. It can show up as a small dread or as a paralyzing and crippling force that renders us helpless mentally, physically, and spiritually. Whatever its manifestations, it's essential that we recognize that fear is a spiritual force that can negatively affect our lives and can only be conquered by a greater spiritual force — our faith in God.

Jesus frequently told people to "fear not." He recognized the devastating effect that fear can have on our faith. Fear can stop the blessings of God from flowing into our lives. It's God's will for us to live a fear-free, faith-filled life every day. If Jesus told us to "fear not," then that means we have the capability to do it. Did you know that "fear not" or variations of the phrase like "do not be afraid" occur 365 times in the Bible? That's one for every day of the year!

But how do we put that directive into practice? We fight fear with faith.

We must immerse ourselves in God's Word, studying it and meditating upon it. As we do this, our understanding of God's love, power, and promises grows, and our faith arises and is fortified. The Word of God is the ultimate weapon against fear, as it continually reminds us of His unfailing faithfulness and protection. Light the fuse of faith in your heart through your mouth.

Conquering fear is an ongoing process, and it may not always be easy. There will be times when fear may seem overwhelming, but we must persevere in our faith, continually leaning on God's promises and His unfailing love. So... When fear tries to come against you, you resist it and Speak the truth in faith saying:

"Jesus has not given me a spirit of fear, but of power and love and a sound mind. I will not be afraid because Jesus said not to. I will remain calm and trust the Lord. *I will not fear.*"

Prayer

Lord, You said in Your Word not to fear because You are with me. You said not to be dismayed because You are my God. You promised to strengthen me and help me. You promised that You would uphold me. You have promised me a spirit of power, love, and a sound mind. Thank You, Father, for Your promises. Thank You for never leaving me. Your words and Your company are precious to me. I ask You now for the strength, help, and sound mind afforded to me in Your Word.

Help me to act not on how I feel in the heat of the moment, or in the cold of the night, but rather to act on what I know to be true in Your Word. When fear threatens to take over my heart and mind, I ask that You step in and remind me of the truth that breaks the chains of fear and doubt in my life. I recognize that fear is an enemy of my heart and mind, and I refuse to let it steal the peace and joy in my life. Give me courage and strength to face the fears in my life that try to hold me captive. You have assured me that You would remain with me in times of trouble and comfort me when fear grips my heart. I choose to trust in You rather than fear my circumstances. You uphold me and sustain me. As I seek Your peace and wisdom, when I am tempted to fear, I will look to You. You have made me secure, capable, and free from fear in my life. I declare now—not by how I feel, but by merit of my faith in Your Word—that I am fearless.

In Jesus' name, amen.

Scriptures

So do not fear, for I am with you; do not be dismayed, for I am your God. I will strengthen you and help you; I will uphold you with my righteous right hand.

—ISAIAH 41:10 (NIV)

Have not I commanded thee? Be strong and of a good courage; be not afraid, neither be thou dismayed: for the LORD thy God is with thee whithersoever thou goest.

—JOSHUA 1:9

The LORD is my light and my salvation; whom shall I fear? the LORD is the strength of my life; of whom shall I be afraid?

—PSALMS 27:1

For God hath not given us the spirit of fear; but of power, and of love, and of a sound mind.

—2 TIMOTHY 1:7

But when I am afraid, I will put my trust in you. I praise God for what he has promised. I trust in God, so why should I be afraid? What can mere mortals do to me?

—PSALM 56:3-4 (NLT)

I sought the Lord, and he heard me, and delivered me from all my fears.

—PSALM 34:4 (KJV)

Thoughts

....
....
....
....
....
....
....
....
....
....
....
....
....
....
....
....
....
....
....
....
....
....
....

"If the Lord be with us, we have no cause of fear. His eye is upon us, His arm over us, His ear open to our prayer, His grace sufficient, His promise unchangeable."

—JOHN NEWTON (Author of the Hymn "Amazing Grace")

In the shadowed vale of sorrow, where despairing thoughts
      do tread,
Lurks the specter of depression, casting doubts and fears widespread.
Like a cloud that veils the sunshine, it obscures the light of day,
Dulling senses, tinting visions in a monochrome array.
Through this dim and darkened lens, life's hues are lost, all joy
      effaced,
Down despair's road, we wander, by encroaching shadows chased.
Yet He whispers, in the throes of life's relentless, grinding mill,
That depression's grip, though iron-strong, is subject to our will.
"Rise!" He urges, against this foe, this thief of peace, this well
      of woe,
"Claim your joy, your soul's release, from this dark beast demand
      a cease!"
For in the Lord, a joy is found, that in our hearts can deeply ground,
Not swayed by life's erratic swing, but firm in faith, to hope we cling.
For not in grief, nor in sadness, does the Lord find His gladness,
But in our joy, midst trials faced, in steadfast faith, His love is traced.
Against depression's crushing tide, with grateful heart, we
      must abide,
Count blessings, speak life's words anew, let scriptures guide
      our view.
Like Paul, in chains, yet rejoiced he stood, in direst times,
      he understood
That joy transcends our circumstance, in God's embrace, we find
      our stance.
So take the helm, let faith steer through, this stormy sea, this
      trial's brew,
For depression's chains, though tight they seem, are naught before
      the faith's bright beam.

—JAKE AND KEITH

4

Depression

Depression is your enemy. It can steal your joy and peace. It can become a cloud that casts a shadow over everything in your life. Depression dulls your senses and causes you to view every area of life through a dark filter. It can take you down a road of despair and discouragement that only leads to worry, fear, and hopelessness.

Some say that depression is a natural response to adverse events or circumstances in our lives. Maybe it seems that way in your life right now, but it doesn't have to stay that way! Did you know that you can choose *not* to be depressed? You can choose to take control of your life back from depression. Find your joy in the Lord instead of living "up" one day and "down" the next. Choose to live by faith instead of letting the circumstances of life dictate how you feel.

It is not God's will for you to be discouraged, down, and depressed. You can choose to be joyful even in the midst of the most difficult situations.

Fight back against depression! Go on the offensive with your thoughts and your words. What are you thankful for? Count your blessings. Go to the Bible and look up scriptures on encouragement and begin to speak them over your life. No matter what situation you find yourself in, you can find something to be thankful for.

This is the key that unlocks the prison of depression.

In the face of adversity, the Apostle Paul serves as an inspiring example of choosing to rejoice even when circumstances seem dire. Despite being imprisoned and facing severe challenges, Paul wrote to the Philippians, "Rejoice in the Lord always. I will say it again: Rejoice!" (Philippians 4:4). Paul's ability to maintain a sense of joy and gratitude even while in prison demonstrates the transformative power and indomitable spirit of faith to the of a Child of God.

God loves you, and He knows what you are going through. He wants to help you. Go to Him in prayer. Cast your cares on Him, because He cares for you. Like Paul, you will find that the prison of depression is no match for the power of God's love, grace, and mercy. Choose to take control of your life back from depression, and let your renewed faith guide you to a future filled with happiness, purpose, and fulfillment.

Prayer

Lord, I thank You that the value of my life was so precious to You that You sent Your own Son to die so that I may have life and enjoy it to the fullest. Depression threatens to devalue that sacrifice by attacking my soul with a darkness that seeks to destroy me from the inside out. The people in my life, my contributions to Your Kingdom and to my fellow man, my wealth, my health, and the general meaning of my life are all under attack when I am battling depression, and so, Father, I humbly ask for Your help.

Help me to overcome depression. I know there is no problem too big, no hurt too deep, and no mistake so terrible that You cannot provide power, love, and wisdom to overcome it. I endeavor to step out on Your Word, to speak and believe what You have said concerning me. Break the power of depression in my life. Restore my joy and the sense of value in my life. Remind me of who I am to You. Help me to trust more in what Your Word says than in how I feel. I cast my cares and worries on You because You care for me. I refuse to let depression control my life. Help me to replace my fears with faith, my doubts with belief, my worries with trust, and my lack of confidence with courage. Show me how to set my mind on the right things, to focus on You and Your promises rather than on my problems. Help me to be thankful for all the things You have provided in my life. Lord, help me to encourage myself in You. Let Your joy be my strength and Your peace fill my soul. Let Your grace and mercy comfort and sustain me.

In Jesus' name, amen.

Scriptures

I waited patiently for the LORD; he inclined to me and heard my cry. He drew me up from the pit of destruction, out of the miry bog, and set my feet upon a rock, making my steps secure. He put a new song in my mouth, a song of praise to our God. Many will see and fear, and put their trust in the LORD.

— PSALMS 40:1-3 (ESV)

Friends, when life gets really difficult, don't jump to the conclusion that God isn't on the job. Instead, be glad that you are in the very thick of what Christ experienced. This is a spiritual refining process, with glory just around the corner.

— 1 PETER 4:12-13 (MSG)

Now it happened, when David and his men came to Ziklag on the third day, that the Amalekites had invaded the South and Ziklag, attacked Ziklag and burned it with fire, and had taken captive the women and those who were there, from small to great; they did not kill anyone, but carried them away and went their way. So David and his men came to the city, and there it was, burned with fire; and their wives, their sons, and their daughters had been taken captive. Then David and the people who were with him lifted up their voices and wept, until they had no more power to weep. And David's two wives, Ahinoam the Jezreelitess, and Abigail the widow of Nabal the Carmelite, had been taken captive. Now David was greatly distressed, for the people spoke of stoning him, because the soul of all the people was grieved, every man for his sons and his daughters. But David strengthened himself in the Lord his God. Then David said to Abiathar the priest, Ahimelech's son, "Please bring the ephod here to me." And Abiathar brought the ephod to David. So David inquired of the Lord, saying, "Shall I pursue this troop? Shall I overtake them?" And He answered him, "Pursue, for you shall surely overtake them and without fail recover all."

— 1 SAMUEL 30:1-8 (NKJV)

Thoughts

Why am I discouraged? Why is my heart so sad? I will put my hope in God! I will praise him again—my Savior and my God!

—Psalm 42:11 (NLT)

Lord, when we long for life without difficulties, remind us that oaks grow strong in contrary winds and diamonds are made under pressure.

—Peter Marshall

"We are hedged in (pressed) on every side [troubled and oppressed in every way], but not cramped or crushed; we suffer embarrassments and are perplexed and unable to find a way out, but not driven to despair; We are pursued (persecuted and hard driven), but not deserted [to stand alone]; we are struck down to the ground, but never struck out and destroyed;"

—2 Corinthians 4:8-9 amp

5

Pressure

We all have to deal with various pressures in our lives: pressure to act, to perform, to conform, to stand out, or to advance. We can even feel pressured to buy things we don't need to impress people we don't know or to fix a troubled marriage or rescue a rebellious teen.

But when the pressure is on, it can distract us so that we don't think clearly. Seldom do we make good decisions or wise choices when we are under pressure. In fact, when you feel the pressure that you have to make a rush decision, that's the very moment when you should back up, take a breath, and *make* yourself take some time to analyze your choices more closely.

The pressures of life can overwhelm us if we let them. So the key is—*don't let them!* When you start to feel the pressure of a situation, turn to God and His Word. The Lord has promised that He will give us wisdom if we will just ask Him.

Refuse to give in to pressure, and instead spend some time in prayer, asking the Lord for wisdom and guidance concerning whatever situation you are facing. It might also be a good idea to get some input from a trusted friend who might have a more objective perspective.

The Bible tells you to cast our cares on God, to trust Him, because He cares for you. He will take what the enemy has meant for evil and turn it into good. With every temptation and pressure, God has promised relief and a way of escape. Refuse to let the pressures of life steal your joy and peace.

As we navigate through life, it is not uncommon for pressures to intensify when we fixate on them. The more we dwell on these burdens, the heavier they become, ultimately reaching a point of unbearable and overwhelming proportions. However, there is a transformative shift that occurs when we redirect our focus from our problems to the Lord. By fixing our gaze on Him and seeking His guidance, we allow ourselves to perceive our challenges through a lens of faith and trust. As we adjust our perspective to recognize God's ever-present hand in our lives, the once-crushing pressures begin to alleviate, making way for a renewed sense of peace and strength to overcome any obstacle that lies ahead.

Prayer

Thank You, Father, for being my sure foundation. When the pressures of this life are at their greatest, when the heat of the fire is intense, and when my circumstances seek to overwhelm me like the rushing of a mighty river, You remain steady. Your Word is unfailing and incorruptible, Your character is perfect and holy, and Your ways are full of wisdom and peace. Your company brings comfort and love for You are the everlasting Rock of Ages. You are my refuge and strength. You are my help in times of trouble.

I ask for what Paul said concerning his situation to also be true concerning my situation: When I am experiencing persecution and I feel pressed on every side, I thank You that the comfort of Your presence would prevent my spirit from being crushed by the weight of the opposition. When the confusion of this world seeks to enter my mind over a perplexing situation, I pray that the truth of Your Word would shatter any and all feelings of despair.

Finally, Lord, I ask for Your help with my emotions in the heat of the moment. I ask for wisdom, clarity, guidance, and the boldness to act when the need is great and the time is short. When I can feel my emotions rise to the surface, I ask that You would help me to stay calm and remind me to quiet my emotions and measure my response with faith and patience. Help me not to feel forced into making rash or hasty decisions, but to rely on You in the moment—or if I am able, to set aside time to seek You in prayer concerning the issue at hand. Thank You, Lord, for hearing my prayer. I trust You, and I will follow Your direction.

In Jesus' name, amen.

Scriptures

We are hard pressed on every side, but not crushed; perplexed, but not in despair; persecuted, but not abandoned; struck down, but not destroyed.

—2 Corinthians 4:8-9 (NIV)

Consider it a sheer gift, friends, when tests and challenges come at you from all sides. You know that under pressure, your faith-life is forced into the open and shows its true colors. So don't try to get out of anything prematurely. Let it do its work so you become mature and well-developed, not deficient in any way.

—James 1:2-4 (MSG)

And we know that all things work together for good to them that love God, to them who are the called according to His purpose.

—Romans 8:28

"Cast your cares on the Lord and he will sustain you; he will never let the righteous be shaken."

—Psalm 55:22 (NIV)

"When you pass through the waters, I will be with you; and through the rivers, they shall not overwhelm you; when you walk through fire you shall not be burned, and the flame shall not consume you."

—Isaiah 43:2 (ESV)

Thoughts

"Pressure is a word that is misused in our vocabulary.
When you start thinking of pressure, it's because you've
started to think of failure."

—TOMMY LASORDA

"When one door closes, another opens; but we often look so long and so regretfully upon the closed door that we do not see the one which has opened for us."
—ALEXANDER GRAHAM BELL

Liberation

When purpose feels questionable,
And you aren't capable,
Your strength fades
As you waver like the field's blades,

Feeling so much to be void of feeling,
Crying tearless staring at the ceiling,
Trapped in a circle of promised change,
While realizing you're poisoned by regret's fang,

There is something you need to hear
Something to spark love's pure tear
Stop trying to run so far,
You're doing better than you think you are,

Jesus came because of His deep love for you.
You matter more than you think you do,
Stop trying to be this and that, just be His
It's less about you than you think it is

—JAKE PROVANCE
Inspired by the Steven Furtick sermon
"The Most Encouraging Message You've Never Heard"

6

Regret

We all have regrets. It is practically impossible to live on this earth for any length of time and have no regrets. The trick is to not let regrets have *you*, because if you are not careful, regret can control you.

Maybe you feel your mistakes have been so big that you don't deserve God's help. Welcome to the crowd! None of us *deserve* it, but by His grace, God has made it available to us. Maybe you've done things that have left you feeling ashamed and hopeless. Past sins that make you feel unworthy or failures that make you feel inadequate can hang over your head. Whatever regrets you have, they bar the doorway of your future. Whenever you want to step out for God, regret can stand in your way, laughing at you.

We've all fallen short with our choices and made mistakes. We've all sinned and messed up. But it's time to get back up and brush yourself off.

God does not hold *any* of your past mistakes and failures against you! When you ask God to forgive you, He throws your sins in the sea of forgetfulness and remembers them no more. It's time for you to do the same! If He has forgiven you, don't you think it's time to forgive yourself?

Do your best to learn from the past, but never let the regrets of the past keep you from pursuing your dreams for the future. With God's help, you can rise above your mistakes. Let's face it—mistakes, failures, and missteps are a part of life.

But regret doesn't have to be a part of your life if you choose to trust in God. When you feel the urge to dwell on past failures, remember to step out in faith, relying on God's grace and guidance. It's important to discern the difference between learning from your past and letting it haunt you. Use your experiences as lessons, allowing them to shape you into a wiser, stronger person, but don't let them dictate your every move or prevent you from embracing the opportunities that lie ahead. By placing your trust in God, you can break free from the chains of regret and confidently move forward, knowing that His love and support will carry you through any challenges that may arise. Embrace the future with an open heart, unburdened by the weight of past mistakes, and let the power of God's grace propel you towards the fulfilling life He has planned for you.

Prayer

Dear Lord, I thank You for Your wonderful grace. I know I don't deserve it, that I could never earn it, and yet You lavish it on me freely. Who is it whose opinions, judgments, and decrees matter more than Yours? There is no one. You alone are the King. So, if You forgive me—if You forget my past sins, mistakes, and embarrassments—then I will not let anyone else, including myself, keep me under the thumb of regret and sorrow. So, Lord, I ask for Your help to forgive myself and let go of my regrets. Help me not to worry or have any frustration or anxiety about the mistakes I have made. If thoughts or feelings rise up from the past and threaten to cripple me, I ask that You would remind me of what You have decreed concerning me. Help me to choose to cast my daily cares and concerns onto You.

I choose now to forget the past and look toward tomorrow with joy and gladness. I ask that Your peace would reside in my heart, in my life, and in my home. Today is a new day for me— with no regrets. No matter how many times I have stumbled in the past, I can start afresh and new in You. I recognize that no amount of regret can change the past, but I know that You can restore anything I may have lost. I ask You to redeem my mistakes and failures and help me to receive Your forgiveness. I trust You to fulfill Your plans and purposes in my life. Lord, I thank You that You have a bright future planned for me.

In Jesus' name, amen.

Scriptures

Brethren, I count not myself to have apprehended: but this one thing I do, forgetting those things which are behind, and reaching forth unto those things which are before.

—PHILIPPIANS 3:13

If we confess our sins, He is faithful and just to forgive us our sins and to cleanse us from all unrighteousness.

—1 JOHN 1:9

Where is the god who can compare with you—wiping the slate clean of guilt, Turning a blind eye, a deaf ear, to the past sins of your purged and precious people? You don't nurse your anger and don't stay angry long, for mercy is your specialty. That's what you love most. And compassion is on its way to us. You'll stamp out our wrong doing. You'll sink our sins to the bottom of the ocean.

—MICAH 7:18-19 (MSG)

There is therefore now no condemnation to those who are in Christ Jesus, who do not walk according to the flesh, but according to the Spirit.

—ROMANS 8:1 (NKJV)

I acknowledged my sin to You, And my iniquity I have not hidden. I said, 'I will confess my transgressions to the Lord,' And You forgave the iniquity of my sin.

—PSALM 32:5 (NKJV)

Thoughts

....

....

....

....

....

....

....

....

....

....

....

....

....

....

....

....

....

....

....

....

....

....

....

"Do not remember the former things, Nor consider the things of old. Behold, I will do a new thing, Now it shall spring forth; Shall you not know it? I will even make a road in the wilderness And rivers in the desert."

—Isaiah 43:18-19 (NKJV)

"If you are stressed by anything external, the pain is not due to the thing itself, but to your estimate of it; and this you have the power to revoke at any moment"

—MARCUS AURELIUS

Are you tired? Worn out? Burned out on religion? Come to me. Get away with me and you'll recover your life. I'll show you how to take a real rest. Walk with me and work with me – watch how I do it. Learn the unforced rhythms of grace. I won't lay anything heavy or ill-fitting on you. Keep company with me and you'll learn to live freely and lightly.

—MATTHEW 11:28-30 MSG

7

Stress

In this day and age, we are no strangers to stress. Mental tension and worry caused by our problems—and life in general—can be a hallmark of daily life. Stress can fuel cancer, shrink the brain, age you prematurely, lead to clinical depression, weaken your immune system, and increase the risk of stroke and heart attack. In short, stress is killing us!

And it's not just the big events in our lives that cause us stress. It's the day-to-day grind we put ourselves through. We live in a fast-paced society where it's common to have an overly-busy schedule. Day in and day out, we sacrifice ourselves for our job, our friends, our hobbies, and our family. You could be a mother being stretched thin by the responsibilities of compassionate care. You may be young with big dreams, enthralled in your studies and carrier development feeling overwhelmed and underprepared for the life ahead. You could be A father trying to provide strength and stability for your family, while feeling like you don't measure up to the role you been entrusted as the leader of your family. You could be a single parent who feels alone, and afraid with the rest of your life spoken for by sacrifice and struggle —if stress is killing you slowly, it's time to put on the brakes.

It's not God's will for you to live a life full of stress. The Bible tell us that we can maintain a sense of peace in our lives. So what do we do to break the stress cycle?

Simply starting your day with a morning devotional and a few minutes of prayer can set the tone for a stress-free day. Listening to worship music and meditating on scriptures throughout the day can help you keep your sanity and maintain a peaceful spirit. Try embarking on your day infused with the peace and joy of God in your heart. It will help you to sail right through those potentially stressful situations with ease and grace.

Stress, in essence, is a response to the external challenges and situations that we encounter in our daily lives. When we experience stress, it is usually connected to a specific thought or circumstance. As we navigate through life, these stressors can accumulate, much like barnacles on a ship, ultimately weighing us down and draining our energy. For believers, the key is to consistently meditate on God's faithfulness and trust in His guidance to handle the problems that arise in the present moment. Instead of fixating on the issues of the past or the uncertainties of the future, we should strive to embrace each day as it comes, focusing on the blessings and opportunities it brings.

When stress attempts to latch onto our lives and thoughts, turning to God and His word provides us with the strength, resilience, and the answers needed to overcome these stresses.

Prayer

Father, thank You for Your peace. Before Jesus ascended on high, He said that He would give us the same peace in which He operated while He was on the earth. I know that the peace that comes from You is the peace that passes all understanding. It doesn't even make sense how I could be so content and filled with peace when others look at all the things I have going on in my life. Lord, I know that the more I look at all the problems and responsibilities I am facing—and the amount of time I have to handle them—the more my stress begins to rise. In contrast, I know that when I look to You, Your Word, and Your ability to help me soar through each and every day, I am filled with joy and peace. So, Lord, I ask for Your help to keep my eyes fixed on You. Help me to keep a watchful eye on the condition of my attitude and mentality concerning my day. Help me to recognize the stress I am experiencing before it gets out of hand so that I may correct my perspective and remain in Your rest and peace.

Lord, help me to live free from stress. Show me how to trust in You and be calm, even when the circumstances of life are screaming so loudly that it's difficult to hear anything else. Let me rise above turmoil and agitation to a place of perfect peace in Your presence. By faith, and in obedience to Your Word, I cast all my cares, all my anxieties, and all my stress on You, and I receive Your peace in exchange. Show me how to develop a calm spirit and the spiritual strength not to let the cares of this world cause frustration or pressure in my life. I choose to worship You and praise You. I purpose to have a grateful heart, no matter what I am going through. With Your help and guidance, I am confident that I can live a stress-free life.

In Jesus' name, amen.

Scriptures

Peace I leave with you, my peace I give unto you: not as the world giveth, give I unto you. Let not your heart be troubled, neither let it be afraid.

—JOHN 14:27

Come unto me, all ye that labour and are heavy laden, and I will give you rest.

—MATTHEW 11:28

These things I have spoken unto you, that in me ye might have peace. In the world ye shall have tribulation: but be of good cheer; I have overcome the world.

—JOHN 16:33

If you work the words into your life, you are like a smart carpenter who dug deep and laid the foundation of his house on bedrock. When the river burst its banks and crashed against the house, nothing could shake it; it was built to last.

—LUKE 6:48 (MSG)

"Therefore do not worry about tomorrow, for tomorrow will worry about itself. Each day has enough trouble of its own."

—MATTHEW 6:34 (NIV)

Thoughts

"The Lord is my shepherd, I lack nothing. He makes me lie down in green pastures, he leads me beside quiet waters, he refreshes my soul."

—Psalm 23:1-3 (NIV)

"The greatest antidote to frustration is a calm faith, not in your own cleverness, or in hard toil, but in God's guidance."

—Norman Vincent Peale

"Our fatigue is often caused not by work, but by worry, frustration and resentment."

—Dale Carnegie

8

Frustration

Life is full of little daily annoyances and frustrations. There are inconsiderate drivers, fast food drive-through clerks who never get your order right, an endless series of red lights when you're in a hurry, the clueless shopper who takes 45 things to the "10 items or less" checkout register, and on and on.

If people are the source of your frustration, then realize that everyone is fighting their own battles and may be facing struggles we know nothing about. By extending grace to others, we not only improve our own emotional well-being, but we also create an atmosphere of kindness that can ripple outward, touching the lives of those around us.

Maybe you face frustration on a higher level — like feeling as though you're stuck in a dead-end job, or trying to get through to a rebellious teen. Perhaps you're frustrated with yourself because you just can't seem to lose weight or stick with that exercise plan. Maybe you can't find the opportunity to spend quality time with your spouse or kids or you feel you are not on the spiritual level you desire. Whatever the source, frustration can keep you agitated, upset, and just no fun to be around.

Take a timeout, gather yourself, and take a deep breath. Consider this: life is undeniably filled with both annoyances and blessings. No amount of money, no special person, nor the perfect job or situation is devoid of various annoyances and frustrations. The key lies in what you choose to focus on. By maintaining an attitude of gratitude and cultivating a lifestyle of thanksgiving, your frustration will melt away like a snowball in the hot August sun. Frustration is but one response among many to an undesirable situation. You can choose to fill your mind and your words with thanksgiving, not for the problems, but for the solution to them: Christ, and the blessings He has already given you. This shift in perspective will cause your irritability and agitation to alleviate; It helps us appreciate the beauty amid the chaos and be ever mindful that God is always with us.

The more mindful you become of God's love for you, ability in you, and companionship with you, Then the less Frustration and stress will influence your heart, mind and decisions.

Prayer

Lord, You said in Your Word that You came to this earth so that we might have life and have it more abundantly. Thank You for not designing a life for me that was meant to tear me down; rather, You have made it clear that You want me to have an abundant and enjoyable life. I delight myself in You, Lord, and I declare that these present troubles are not worthy enough to hold my attention.

Father, I ask for Your help. I know that if I am frustrated, then my thoughts are not set on You. If I'm irritated and agitated, then I'm not focusing on the good. Help me to maintain my composure when things aren't going my way. Help me to trust in You, to lean on Your wisdom and strength to put a smile back on my face and address the problem at hand with Your help. Allow me to be patient with myself and with others. When life becomes hectic and demanding, show me how not to let frustration rob my peace and steal my joy.

Lord, help me to maintain a peaceful spirit and a good attitude even when the circumstances around me are not ideal. When faced with challenges and obstacles in my life, help me face them with a resolute determination. Empower me to press on with confidence, knowing You have promised to give me strength to overcome any situation. When things don't go as expected, help me to remain calm, trusting in You and not giving in to frustration. Grant me clarity of thought, mental focus, and ideal comprehension. Give me wisdom and guidance on how to navigate through the storms of life and arrive at a place of complete victory. I will not be unsettled, distraught, or frustrated. Instead, Your peace will rule in my life.

In Jesus' name, amen.

Scriptures

Understand this, my dear brothers and sisters: You must all be quick to listen, slow to speak, and slow to get angry.

—JAMES 1:19 (NLT)

Let us not lose heart in doing good, for in due time we will reap if we do not grow weary.

—GALATIANS 6:9 (NASB)

The LORD shall fight for you, and ye shall hold your peace.

—EXODUS 14:14

Delight thyself also in the LORD: and he shall give thee the desires of thine heart.

—PSALM 37:4

For I reckon that the sufferings of this present time are not worthy to be compared with the glory which shall be revealed in us.

—ROMANS 8:18

"For our present troubles are small and won't last very long. Yet they produce for us a glory that vastly outweighs them and will last forever! So we don't look at the troubles we can see now; rather, we fix our gaze on things that cannot be seen. For the things we see now will soon be gone, but the things we cannot see will last forever."

—2 CORINTHIANS 4:17-18 (NLT)

Thoughts

"The greatest discovery of my generation is that a human being can alter his life by altering his attitudes."

—WILLIAM JAMES

"Finish each day and be done with it. You have done what you could. Some blunders and absurdities no doubt crept in; forget them as soon as you can. Tomorrow is a new day. You shall begin it serenely and with too high a spirit to be encumbered with your old nonsense."

—Ralph Waldo Emerson

"I want you to start a crusade in your life—to dare to be your best. I maintain that you are a better, more capable person than you have demonstrated so far. The only reason you are not the person you should be is you don't dare to be. Once you dare, once you stop drifting with the crowd and face life courageously, life takes on a new significance. New forces take shape within you. New powers harness themselves for your service."

—Excerpt from *I Dare You* by
William Danforth

9

Self-Criticism

So often we can be our own worst enemies. We set unrealistic expectations for ourselves and are critical of ourselves when we don't live up to them. But self-criticism is a destructive process that can undermine what God wants to accomplish in our lives.

It's time to borrow a page from God's playbook and give yourself some grace. We are all works in progress. We all make mistakes, we all drop the ball, and we all fall short. *So what?* When you miss the mark, get up, dust yourself off, and get back in the game.

That's not to make light of the fact that there is always room for improvement, and yes, we should make a habit of evaluating our own lives. Everyone needs to make adjustments at times to get back on track to living a more fulfilled and productive life, but there is a big difference between self-*evaluation* and self-*criticism*. Self-evaluation is a constructive, beneficial exercise that helps us recognize the areas where we need to improve. On the other hand, self-criticism is a destructive force that can lead to discouragement, discontent, and depression.

So instead of tearing ourselves down, we should build ourselves up by thinking, speaking, and acting on God's Word. God is not in Heaven criticizing you; He is at the head of a great crowd of witnesses cheering you on! God's Word has strength, direction, and promises for you—if you will seek them out. Ask the Lord to help you in areas you need to improve. By His Spirit and through His Word, you can accomplish anything.

Often the source of our self-criticism is due to comparison. It's common for us to fall into the trap of comparing ourselves to others. However, this can lead to an unstable self-image, as it constantly fluctuates based on the actions of those around us, causing us to feel inadequate or insecure in the face of others' accomplishments or successes. Instead, we should remember that God's love for us is unwavering and constant. By focusing on who God says we can and should be, we establish a solid foundation for self-improvement and growth. Trust in His guidance and lean on His help throughout our journey to become the best version of ourselves. Even when we fall short, God's grace allows us the opportunity to learn, grow, and try again with renewed determination.

Prayer

Thank You, Father, for all the wonderful things You have spoken to me and over my life. You sent Your Son to die for me, declaring my immense value to You. You've freed me from sin and bondage. You've made me a new creature, and You have declared me Your child. Thank You. Father, I ask for Your help to see myself the way that You see me: complete, strong, and Your beloved child. Help me not to strive to attain something that I already possess. You've made me worthy to be in Your presence just as I am; help me not to avoid coming to You until I feel like I've "earned" it by something I do. Christ is the only reason I am worthy to come boldly to You, and I ask You to help me maintain that boldness even when my actions are anything but holy and right.

Father, I want to see myself as You see me. Help me to learn how to evaluate myself—my thoughts and actions—so that I can improve without falling into self-criticism or condemnation. Help me to forgive myself just as You have forgiven me. Let me not be overly critical about my shortcomings, but instead show me how to love myself without becoming self-absorbed. Help me to not spend the majority of my time thinking about myself, good or bad, but rather, to focus on You and how I can benefit others. Give me grace and mercy to know that I am a work in progress and to learn how to navigate growth without harsh judgment. When I make a mistake, help me not to get down on myself. Teach me not to get discouraged or lose heart when I miss the mark. You said You would never condemn me. Help me to follow Your example. Teach me to encourage myself in You, and give me the confidence to live my life free from self-criticism and condemnation. Continue the good work You have started in me and help me to complete that work in my life.

In Jesus' name, amen.

Scriptures

Let no corrupt communication proceed out of your mouth, but that which is good to the use of edifying, that it may minister grace unto the hearers.

—EPHESIANS 4:29

All scripture is given by inspiration of God, and is profitable for doctrine, for reproof, for correction, for instruction in righteousness:

—2 TIMOTHY 3:16

Fight the good fight of the faith. Take hold of the eternal life to which you were called and about which you made the good confession in the presence of many witnesses.

—1 TIMOTHY 6:12 (ESV)

Sin is no longer your master, for you no longer live under the requirements of the law. Instead, you live under the freedom of God's grace.

—ROMANS 6:14 (NLT)

"Search me, O God, and know my heart; test me and know my anxious thoughts. See if there is any offensive way in me, and lead me in the way everlasting."

—PSALM 139:23-24 (NIV)

Thoughts

"Self-criticism, like self-administered brain surgery, is perhaps not a wise idea."

—JOYCE CAROL OATES

"No one can make you feel inferior without your consent"
—ELEANOR ROOSEVELT

People are illogical, unreasonable, and self-centered
Love them anyway
If you do good, people will accuse you of selfish
ulterior motives.
Do good anyway
If you are successful, you will win false friends and
true enemies.
Succeed anyway
The good you do today will be forgotten tomorrow
Do good anyway
Honesty and frankness make you vulnerable.
Be honest and frank anyway
The biggest men and women with the biggest ideas can be shot
down by the smallest men and women with the smallest minds.
Think big anyway
People favor underdogs but follow only top dogs.
Fight for a few underdogs anyway
What you spend years building may be destroyed overnight
Build anyway
People really need help but may attack you if you do help them
Help people anyway
Give the world the best you have and you'll get kicked in
the teeth.
Give the world the best you have anyway

—THE PARADOXICAL COMMANDMENTS by
KENT M. KEITH, Was proudly displayed in
Mother Teresa's Calcutta's children's home

10

Seeking the Approval of Others

We all like to be appreciated. Psychologists tell us that it is one of the greatest desires in every individual. If you are honest with yourself, you will admit that you enjoy being appreciated—we all do. Whether it's a pat on the back from your boss, a handshake of appreciation from your pastor, or a simple "thanks, Mom" from your child for making pancakes for breakfast, we all want to be appreciated. Appreciation provides us with a sense of purpose, and it is one of the most powerful motivators.

But we get into dangerous territory when we begin to rely on the approval of others to determine our self-worth or the level of joy in our life. We can begin to volunteer at church so everyone will see what good Christians we are. We can pray with a little more zeal to show friends how spiritual we are. We can try to be the perfect parent and spouse in public so people will notice and recognize our accomplishments. If we are not careful, we may find ourselves doing the right things—for the wrong reasons. In our unhealthy quest for the approval of others, we often find ourselves in a situation where we might compromise our core beliefs just to avoid causing offense. This behavior can lead us down a path that erodes the very foundation of our faith, as we prioritize the opinions of others over the convictions God has placed within us. As Billy Graham once said, "Our society strives to avoid any possibility of offending anyone – except God." It is vital that we recognize the danger in this mindset and strive to uphold our beliefs, even if it means facing disapproval or criticism from others. In doing so, we will not only stay true to ourselves and our faith, but we will also be an example to those around us, showing them the strength and integrity that comes from a life firmly grounded in God's truth. If you start viewing your importance, your ability, and your worth the way you think those around you view it, it's time for a change.

If you are constantly seeking the approval of others to determine your happiness, you will find yourself living a very unhappy life. If you put too much emphasis on what others think, you may make decisions based on how you think others will respond, not based on your own purpose, destiny, desires, or God's Word.

In the end, let us focus on seeking God's approval rather than that of others, for His love is unchanging and everlasting. By doing so, we will find true contentment and purpose, living a life that is both fulfilling and anchored in His unwavering grace.

Prayer

Lord, thank You for sticking with me—closer even than a brother.

*I ask for Your help not to live my life as a people pleaser. I want to be a light to the world, to brighten many people's day, but I don't want that to be what I live for, nor do I want it to be how I determine my impact and worth in this life. Father, I want to please **You** above all. I want to seek **Your** approval above all. I don't want to pray, give, work, volunteer, or do anything else in this life to garner the adoration of other people. When I pray, I desire to pray because of the intimacy we share. When I give, I want it to be out of a heart overflowing with gratitude for what You have given to me. When I volunteer, I want it to be for Your sake and not mine. When I love, I want it to be because You have first loved me. I know that there is selfishness in me, and plenty of opportunities for me to stray from what You desire, so I ask for Your help in making me genuine in my motives and pure in my intentions.*

Help me not to let the criticism or the insults of others offend me or hurt my feelings. Help me to be more sensitive to Your guidance and direction than the voices of others. Let me have the confidence in myself and in You so that I won't feel the need to strive for the approval of others. Let my greatest desire and goal be to live my life in a way that honors You. I choose to conduct my life with integrity and purpose, based on the principles of Your Word and not on the opinions of others. Help me to be open to the advice and counsel of others, but strong enough to follow the leading of Your Spirit in my heart.

In Jesus' name, amen.

Scriptures

Am I now trying to win the approval of human beings, or of God? Or am I trying to please people? If I were still trying to please people, I would not be a servant of Christ.

—GALATIANS 1:10 (NIV)

The fear of man bringeth a snare: but whoso putteth his trust in the LORD shall be safe.

—PROVERBS 29:25

But just as we have been approved by God to be entrusted with the gospel, so we speak, not to please man, but to please God who tests our hearts

—1 THESSALONIANS 2:4 (ESV)

"When you do something for someone else, don't call attention to yourself. You've seen them in action, I'm sure—'playactors' I call them—treating prayer meeting and street corner alike as a stage, acting compassionate as long as someone is watching, playing to the crowds. They get applause, true, but that's all they get. When you help someone out, don't think about how it looks. Just do it—quietly and unobtrusively. That is the way your God, who conceived you in love, working behind the scenes, helps you out. And when you come before God, don't turn that into a theatrical production either. All these people making a regular show out of their prayers, hoping for fifteen minutes of fame! Do you think God sits in a box seat? Here's what I want you to do: Find a quiet, secluded place so you won't be tempted to role-play before God. Just be there as simply and honestly as you can manage. The focus will shift from you to God, and you will begin to sense his grace."

—MATTHEW 6:2-6 (MSG)

Thoughts

"When we learn to say a deep, passionate yes to the things that really matter, then peace begins to settle onto our lives like golden sunlight sifting to a forest floor."

—THOMAS KINKADE

"The sea is dangerous and its storms are terrible, but these obstacles have never been sufficient reason to remain ashore. Unlike the mediocre, intrepid spirits seek victory over those things that seem impossible. It is with an iron will that they embark on the most daring of all endeavors, to meet the shadowy future without fear and conquer the unknown."

—Written in 1520, By the great explorer
FERDINAND MAGELLAN

"There is no good reason why we should fear the future, but there is every reason why we should face it seriously, neither hiding from ourselves the gravity of the problems before us nor fearing to approach these problems with the unbending, unflinching purpose to solve them aright."

—TEDDY ROOSEVELT

11

Fear of the Future

In the quiet of our thoughts, where the world's clamor fades into a whisper, we often find ourselves confronting the shadow of an uncertain future. It's a shadow cast long and dark by the relentless stream of news that speaks in tones of impending doom. We hear it daily: our economy dances precariously on the edge of collapse, our families are portrayed as losing their moral compass, and our personal security — both financial and emotional — appears as fragile as glass.

This narrative of fear, woven intricately into the fabric of our daily lives, breeds a sense of impending crisis. It's in the air we breathe, in the stories we share, and in the silent, uneasy glances at the future. We are told, in no uncertain terms, that war could erupt at any moment, that diseases, both old and new, lurk around every corner, waiting to strike. Dreams and aspirations, which should light up our path, seem overshadowed by these colossal fears, rendering them distant and unattainable.

Yet, in the midst of this unsettling portrayal of our world, there lies a deeper truth, often forgotten but infinitely powerful. This truth speaks not of helplessness, but of resilience; not of despair, but of hope. Hope is the expectation of a bright tomorrow bases on your faith in God today. The same one who holds today in his hands, will be there tomorrow when you need Him. It this hope that reminds us that the future, while unknown, is a canvas upon which we can paint with our faith the aspirations and dreams God has put in our Hearts. The challenges we face, both personal and global, are but chapters in a larger story — a story that we are writing every day with our thoughts, actions, and beliefs.

To change one's life requires more than rejecting the fear-mongering narrative; it requires a fundamental shift in our heart's posture. It asks us to look beyond the headlines, to find strength in vulnerability, and to embrace the uncertainty of the future as an opportunity for growth and transformation. In doing so, we rediscover the power of hope, the strength of our shared covenant with our Father, and the limitless potential of His spirit at work with in us to overcome, to adapt, and to thrive.

So, Let Hope be kindled in your heart once again, not as passive wishful thinking, but as an active, vibrant, and expectant force that colors your every day with the hues of faith and possibilities. Walk through the minefields of doubt, worry and fear with the quiet assurance that no matter how dark the night, the dawn is always on the horizon. While the World spouts doom and doubt, The word of God speaks of Light, Love, and Life. Let Faith act as it as a craftsman's tool, precise and sure, skillfully carving out a future that aligns with your deepest convictions and values. This faith is your shield and your guide, helping you navigate through life's complexities with a heart full of courage and a spirit of perseverance. This is not a journey of escape from reality, but rather a bold step into living a life defined not by fear, but by the courageous pursuit of a future we create through faith and hope in God.

Prayer

Lord, I thank You for what You have revealed to me in Your Word. You have told me what You have planned for me. They are plans filled with hope and good things. They are plans for a long life of prosperity. You have promised me that my future, like my present, will be filled with Your companionship. I may not know all the specific details of what will come, but I know the One who does, and He is near and dear to me. Thank You, Father, for being my Father and my Friend. Father, I know by faith the thoughts and plans that await me, and I now ask for Your help to believe and act on it daily.

Kindle a passion in my heart to pursue the course that You have prepared for me. Help me to seek out the right people and influences in my life. Help me to recognize the proper path to follow You toward the future You desire for me. If I begin to lose my way or become distracted, I ask for Your mercy and help to set me back on track. I believe that Your grace is bigger than any and all mistakes I have made or could ever make.

Lord, I ask that You would fulfill Your plans and purposes in my life. Help me to be obedient to whatever Your will is for me. Lead, guide, and direct my steps. Give me courage and strength to overcome any obstacle that stands between me and the destiny You have for me. Give me patience and persistence. Let me not lose heart or give up when I face setbacks, but rather to be bold and strong in my faith. Give me fortitude to press on when I am tempted to give up and quit. May my life be a testimony of Your love, Your passion, and Your abundant provision.

In Jesus' name I pray, amen.

Scriptures

Be strong. Take courage. Don't be intimidated. Don't give them a second thought because God, your God, is striding ahead of you. He's right there with you. He won't let you down; he won't leave you.

—DEUTERONOMY 31:6 (MSG)

Trust in the LORD with all thine heart; and lean not unto thine own understanding. In all thy ways acknowledge him, and he shall direct thy paths.

—PROVERBS 3:5-6

"For I know the plans I have for you," declares the Lord, "plans to prosper you and not to harm you, plans to give you hope and a future."

—JEREMIAH 29:11(NIV)

"Therefore I say to you, do not worry about your life, what you will eat or what you will drink; nor about your body, what you will put on. Is not life more than food and the body more than clothing? Look at the birds of the air, for they neither sow nor reap nor gather into barns; yet your heavenly Father feeds them. Are you not of more value than they? Which of you by worrying can add one cubit to his stature?

So why do you worry about clothing? Consider the lilies of the field, how they grow: they neither toil nor spin; and yet I say to you that even Solomon in all his glory was not arrayed like one of these. Now if God so clothes the grass of the field, which today is, and tomorrow is thrown into the oven, will He not much more clothe you, O you of little faith?

Therefore do not worry, saying, 'What shall we eat?' or 'What shall we drink?' or 'What shall we wear?' For after all these things the Gentiles seek. For your heavenly Father knows that you need all these things. But seek first the kingdom of God and His righteousness, and all these things shall be added to you. Therefore do not worry about tomorrow, for tomorrow will worry about its own things. Sufficient for the day is its own trouble."

—MATTHEW 6:25-34 (NKJV)

Thoughts

"The greatest mistake you can make in life is continually fearing that you'll make one."

—ELBERT HUBBARD

Abraham Lincoln's many "Setbacks", on his way to his greatest Triumph.

1831 - Lost his job (**setback**)

1832 - Defeated in run for Illinois State Legislature
(**setback**)

1833 - Failed in business (**setback**)
- Elected to Illinois State Legislature (**success**)

1835 - Sweetheart died (**setback**)

1836 - Had nervous breakdown (**setback**)

1838 - Defeated in run for Illinois House Speaker
(**setback**)

1843 - Defeated in run for nomination for U.S. Congress
(**setback**)

1846 - Elected to Congress (**success**)

1848 - Lost re-nomination (**setback**)

1849 - Rejected for land officer position (**setback**)

1854 - Defeated in run for U.S. Senate (**setback**)

1856 - Defeated in run for nomination for Vice President
(**setback**)

1858 - Again defeated in run for U.S. Senate (**setback**)

1860 - Elected President (**success**)

12

Unexpected Setbacks

When life presents unexpected challenges and setbacks in the pursuit of your dreams, your financial stability, relationships, or family affairs, remember that you are stepping into the fiery crucible of faith. It's at these junctures that your resilience and perseverance are put to the test. When the proverbial punch hits you squarely between the eyes, when the results deviate from your meticulous plans, when years of hard work seemingly disintegrate overnight, it is then that you are faced with a critical choice.

I was faced with one such choice 6 days after My family moved into our brand-new House. A fire broke out in our attic. Guests were staying with us, and we were all panicked as we rushed to escape the blaze. Fortunately, everyone made it out safely. We huddled together on the sidewalk and watched the firemen battle the fire. As smoke and orange-red flames poured out of the building, we knew that all of our stuff inside would likely be damaged or lost. My wife looked at me with tears in her eyes and said, "Okay, mister. What is good about this?" I looked around at her, our kids, and our guests—we were all safe and sound. I answered, "What is good about this? Everyone I love is standing on this sidewalk with me!" Though this situation was terrible, I recognized the good in spite of the obvious bad, seeing the situation for what it really was, a setback in my journey with my family and the Lord.

In labeling these circumstances as 'setbacks', you're inherently acknowledging them not as terminal, but merely bends in the road. Therein lies the silver lining. It's a call to pivot, a nudge to navigate the turn. Round the corner, veer off the beaten path if you must, but never, even for a fleeting second, surrender the divine purpose that has been sowed in your heart.

As you journey through life, continue to dream, achieve, and discover. Momentary afflictions, failures, and setbacks are part and parcel of your voyage. Don't allow them to rattle your spirit; instead, rise above and conquer them.

Moreover, it's worth remembering that these setbacks often hold lessons in disguise, and are catalysts for growth and transformation. These trials can strengthen your resolve, deepen your empathy, and reveal your true mettle. While they may cloud your vision temporarily, remain steadfast in your belief that every stumbling block is a stepping stone towards a larger, more meaningful triumph. For through overcoming adversity, you come to appreciate not just the sweetness of success, but the journey that led you there.

Prayer

Lord, I thank You that You—the One who has begun a good work within me—will continue to perform it until I am meet You face-to-face in heaven. I am grateful that, despite any setbacks in this life—whether from my own failures, attacks by adversaries, or sheer chance—the outcome will ultimately be victory, for You are with me. You are the Alpha and the Omega, the Author and the Finisher of my faith. You said that many are the afflictions of the righteous, but that You will deliver us out of them all.

Help me to realize that setbacks are normal to life here on this earth, but that I should not be upset, because with the trouble comes Your help and with the affliction comes Your deliverance. So, let me not be fearful, anxious, or overwhelmed because of any setbacks I face, but enable me to lean on You and rely on You and Your strength to see me through any situation. Help me not to be discouraged or resentful and not to dwell on the past, but rather to anticipate and look toward the future with hope and expectation. Show me how to turn my setbacks into comebacks; to consider it all joy and treat these challenges as opportunities to be an overcomer and prove for all to see the truth of Your Word. If there are any lessons to learn, reveal to me what I need to know; and then give me guidance and wisdom to move forward with confidence in the pursuit of Your plan for my future. I refuse to let setbacks or failures defeat me or define me. I put my trust in You, Lord, and I have confidence that You will direct my steps and bring to fruition Your plan and purpose for my life.

In Jesus' name, amen.

Scriptures

Many are the afflictions of the righteous: but the LORD delivered him out of them all.

—PSALMS 34:19

Being confident of this very thing, that he which hath begun a good work in you will perform it until the day of Jesus Christ.

—PHILIPPIANS 1:6

For a righteous man falls seven times and rises again, but the wicked stumble in times of calamity.

—PROVERBS 24:16 (ESV)

But those who hope in the LORD will renew their strength. They will soar on wings like eagles; they will run and not grow weary, they will walk and not be faint.

—ISAIAH 40:31(NIV)

Consider it pure joy, my brothers and sisters, whenever you face trials of many kinds, because you know that the testing of your faith produces perseverance. Let perseverance finish its work so that you may be mature and complete, not lacking anything."

—JAMES 1:2-4 (NIV)

Therefore everyone who hears these words of mine and puts them into practice is like a wise man who built his house on the rock. The rain came down, the streams rose, and the winds blew and beat against that house; yet it did not fall, because it had its foundation on the rock. But everyone who hears these words of mine and does not put them into practice is like a foolish man who built his house on sand. The rain came down, the streams rose, and the winds blew and beat against that house, and it fell with a great crash.

—MATTHEW 7:24-27 (NIV)

Thoughts

"The ultimate measure of a man is not where he stands in moments of comfort and convenience, but where he stands at times of challenge and controversy."

—Martin Luther King Jr.

"There is no medicine like hope,
no incentive so great, and no tonic
so powerful as expectation of
something better tomorrow"

—ORISON MARDEN

"A Christian will part with anything rather
than his hope; he knows that hope will keep
the heart both from aching and breaking,
from fainting and sinking; he knows that
hope is a beam of God, a spark of glory, and
that nothing shall extinguish it till the soul be
filled with glory."

—THOMAS BROOKS

13

Hope

For a Christian, there exists no circumstance devoid of hope. Jesus is Loving enough and has enough power to in see you through any conflict or trial. There is not a surer hope, a more solid foundation to put your confidence in, than Him. Hope is not just wishful thinking, Hope is an expectant and confident trust in God; His word, His ability, His willingness, and in His very nature.

When all else fails, when all you can see are the storms, when the world around you is a whirlwind of chaos, do not place your entire hope in people, professions, organizations, or worldly systems. While God may work through some of these people, it is In Him our hope must rest because all these are all subject to change in an instant While God is everlasting and unchanging in His word and Nature.

As you walk the path of life, you may face steep hills and rough terrains. There may be moments when you stumble, fall, and lose your way. You may feel alone, hopeless, and unsteady. Fear and doubt may constantly be knocking at the door to your heart. Weariness and stress make seek to push you to your breaking point. Yet, amidst the raging torrent of darkness arrayed against you, Quiet your heart and mind, fix your gaze upon God and His Word, Lay at his feet all that is weighing heavy on you, and be still.

You'll find His hope is more than just an abstract concept. It's a tangible, life-giving force that will guide you, uphold you, and see you through. It is the light that breaks forth and dawn. You do not walk this life alone, allow the confident expectation on God create and unwavering, light-producing, Solid foundation for you to build your Life upon. Let every step you take be a testament to your hope in Him, your trust in His plans, and your faith in His love.

Allow His light to shine through the cracks in your heart. Allow His grace to mend the broken pieces of your life. No matter how deeply you've been wounded or how far you've strayed, His hope extends to you. His love encompasses every part of your life - the good, the bad, the messy. And in this love, there is endless hope.

Keep your hope in Jesus, and you'll find the strength to face tomorrow. Keep your hope in Him, and you'll discover joy that outlasts the sorrows, peace that surpasses understanding, and love that never fails. Keep your hope in Him, and you'll live an empowered, inspired, and victorious life. No matter what you face, always put your hope in Jesus!

Prayer

Lord, no matter what I see or what I experience in this life, I always have a reason to confidently expect good things because of who You are. I thank You for Your hope—both for a bright future on the earth and a glorious eternity in heaven with You. You are the God of hope, and I ask that You would fill me with all joy and peace through my daily walk of faith with You, so that by the power of the Holy Spirit, I would abound and overflow with hope. Father, I ask that Your overflowing hope would spill out into the lives of those around me. Let me be a bright light in situations of doubt and despair. I ask for Your help in anchoring my soul on You and Your Word as the bedrock of my life. When others may be frightened, depressed, or confused about what the future may hold, I ask that You would use me as a mouthpiece for Your hope and stability, to speak of the expectant future You have promised to those who love You and follow Your ways. To be that light and mouthpiece of hope, I first must have it settled within me the hope that I have set my heart upon in You.

So, Father, I ask You to help me not to lose hope in any circumstance. Help me to focus on You and Your Word and not on the challenges or circumstances I face in this life. Remind me to put my confidence in You and not in this world's system or in the wisdom of men. I trust You, Lord, to sustain me and lift me up. I know that You love me and You will never abandon me, forcing me to face my problems alone. You are my refuge and my shelter from the storms of this life. As I study and meditate on the promises in Your Word, I thank You that my heart is encouraged and my soul is refreshed. I find renewed hope and comfort in Your presence.

In Jesus' name, amen.

Scriptures

The Lord taketh pleasure in them that fear him, in those that
hope in his mercy.

—Psalm 147:11

Never lag in zeal and in earnest endeavor; be aglow and burning
with the Spirit, serving the Lord. Rejoice and exult in hope; be
steadfast and patient in suffering and tribulation; be constant
in prayer.

—Romans 12:11, 12 (AMP)

Wait and hope for and expect the Lord; be brave and of good
courage and let your heart be stout and enduring. Yes, wait for
and hope for and expect the Lord.

—Psalm 27:14 (AMP)

Who by him do believe in God, that raised him up from the dead,
and gave him glory; that your faith and hope might be in God.

—1 Peter 1:21

May the God of your hope so fill you with all joy and peace
in believing [through the experience of your faith] that by the
power of the Holy Spirit you may abound and be overflowing
(bubbling over) with hope.

—Romans 15:13 (AMPC)

Thoughts

"In the midst of winter, I found there was, within me, an invincible summer. And that makes me happy. For it says that no matter how hard the world pushes against me, within me, there's something stronger—something better, pushing right back."

—ALBERT CAMUS

It's the definition of God,

The very reason we were spared from his rod.

Instead he gave us his son,

And in death the job was done,

When the pain of living is high,

And it's tough to muster a sigh,

When your heart is vacant of care,

And the weight too much to bare,

When this whole thing we call life feels

like a loss,

It's time you remembered it wasn't nails

that held him to the cross,

It was the greatest strength clothed in

purity like a dove,

The most beautiful and rare element

called Love.

—By Jake Provance

14

Love

Immerse yourself in a truth that echoes through all creation, a singular characteristic that has defined God's very being—Love. Envision the Bible not simply as a tome of divine words, nor as an important historical document, but as God's heartfelt letter to mankind. Every miracle crafted, every word spoken, every action performed, every contact forged between God and man was driven by one underlying motive: Love. It is the canvas on which the grand narrative of our existence is painted.

Consider our origins, meticulously created in His image. This alone bears testimony to God's desire to nurture children of His own. Yet, we faltered and sowed the seeds of chaos. Unyieldingly, He chose not to abandon us to the wilderness of our transgressions. In an act of unfathomable love, He sent His Son to sacrifice Himself, redeeming us from our own folly.

Let this truth resonate within you: God's love for you is unwavering, etched in the very essence of existence. It's an affection so profound, it transcends mortal comprehension. With an artisan's precision, He wove you in your mother's womb, familiar with the intricate arrangement of each strand of hair on your head. He holds a blueprint for your life, intricately detailed with a purpose uniquely yours. His steadfast promise to never forsake you remains unbroken. Accepting

Christ's sacrifice in your stead heralds your adoption into His divine family. Let not a fleeting moment of doubt cast a shadow over this love. For God is love personified. Soak in the depths of His affection, allowing the essence of faith and love imbued in every word of Scripture to saturate your heart.

Upon this realization, an astounding transformation occurs. Your heart, brimming with God's love, cascades this divine affection onto those around you. A testament to the truth in Jesus' words, "By this everyone will know that you are my disciples, if you love one another."

In His profound wisdom, Jesus distilled the complex mosaic of the law into two fundamental edicts - both deeply rooted in love: 'Love the Lord your God with all your heart, soul, and mind,' the foremost commandment. The second, no less significant, urges, 'Love your neighbor as yourself.'

Observe how Jesus emphasizes loving your neighbor as you would yourself. It insinuates a crucial premise - love for oneself, reflecting the divine affection God holds for you. The world may offer a multitude of definitions for love, presenting varying perspectives on its significance. Yet, God has given his definition of love in His Word in 1 Corinthians 13:

"Love embodies patience and kindness; it does not harbor jealousy or pride. It refrains from arrogance, rudeness, and selfishness. Love bears no irritability, nor does it hold on to resentment. It rejects injustice, rejoicing instead in the truth. Love bears, believes, hopes, and endures all things. Indeed, love never fails."

Meditate on these truths, for they are the heart of God's message to us all: His Love.

Prayer

Heavenly Father, I thank You for loving me so much that You would send Your Son, Jesus, to die on the cross in order to buy me back from my own sins and mistakes. Thank You for loving me even when I am unlovely, even when I make mistakes, even when I mess up, and even when I fail You. Thank You for loving me first and drawing me back to You with Your immeasurable love. Truly there is no love that compares to Yours. Thank You for creating me, for numbering the hairs on my head, for knitting me together in my mother's womb. Truly no one cares for me and knows me as deeply as You do. You see everything about me. All that I am is laid bare before You. In all my nakedness—with my sin, selfishness, doubt, and problems exposed to the light of Your gaze—still You love me. I know You love me truly, which means that You aim to help me grow up and mature, changing from who I am, ridding myself of all the bondage and suffering that sin, selfishness, and doubt has tried to bring into my life.

I ask for Your help to obey Your Word, Your desires for my life. Continue to love me and help me to change into a picture of that same love for others. Help me to trust in Your unconditional love, to know that no matter what I do, Your love for me will never change. Help me to grasp the great love You have for me. Fill my heart with Your love for humanity and help me express Your love to others. Allow me to shine Your love, Your light, and Your life through my life to those around me. Let Your love be the life force that sustains me in difficult times and guides me when I am unsure what to do. Help me to love You with all my heart, all my soul, and all my strength, and to love others as You have loved me. Thank You, Lord, for Your boundless love.

In Jesus' name, amen.

Scriptures

So now faith, hope, and love abide, these three; but the greatest of these is love.

—1 CORINTHIANS 13:13 (ESV)

For God so greatly loved and dearly prized the world that He [even] gave up His only begotten (unique) Son, so that whoever believes in (trusts in, clings to, relies on) Him shall not perish (come to destruction, be lost) but have eternal (everlasting) life.

—JOHN 3:16 (AMP)

We love him, because he first loved us..

—1 JOHN 4:19

By this shall all men know that ye are my disciples, if ye have love one to another.

—JOHN 13:35

"Though I speak with the tongues of men and of angels, but have not love, I have become sounding brass or a clanging cymbal. And though I have the gift of prophecy, and understand all mysteries and all knowledge, and though I have all faith, so that I could remove mountains, but have not love, I am nothing. And though I bestow all my goods to feed the poor, and though I give my body to be burned, but have not love, it profits me nothing."

—1 CORINTHIANS 13:1-3 (NKJV)

Thoughts

"There is no pit so deep that God's love is not deeper still."

—CORRIE TEN BOOM (Holocaust survivor)

"There is an unquenchable fire within us, the power of the Holy Spirit, providing strength in times of distress, a heavenly flame, a lantern glowing in the darkest of hours."

—JOHN WESLEY

"You gain strength, courage and confidence by every experience in which you really stop to look fear in the face. You are able to say to yourself, 'I have lived through this horror. I can take the next thing that comes along.' You must do the thing you think you cannot do."

—ELEANOR ROOSEVELT

15

Strength

Life is a journey that inherently carries with it two distinct elements. The first, Is the drain of the ceaseless cycles presented in everyday life, with its trials and tribulations slowly chipping away at our vitality. Often, it is not just the physical depletion but also the mental exhaustion that stems from worry, anxiety, and frustration. These harbingers of despair stealthily creep into your life, draining your vigor until you're left feeling utterly spent, nursing the wounds of a battle fought with every sunrise.

Where ever your battle field may be, a workplace teeming with strife, the pressure of unemployment, marital turmoil, parenting catastrophes, a serious illness, or the relentless onslaught of daily responsibilities, combatting the fatigue that seeps into our lives while juggling multiple roles requires an inner strength that is often hard to summon. But remember, just as life holds the power to drain, it equally possesses the capacity to replenish.

The pertinent question then arises, "How does one retain their fortitude amid the relentless onslaught of life's challenges?"

The answer to this lies beautifully articulated in God's Word, shedding light on the source of our strength: "Finally, be strong in the Lord and in his mighty power." (Ephesians 6:10 NIV). This strength is a force that is invigorated and fortified through our union with Him. We find our power replenished through Him, tapping into the limitless reservoir of His might.

Aligning your mind with God's Word, anchoring your attention to Him, becomes akin to opening the floodgates to His strength, allowing it to surge into you, infusing your circumstances with divine resilience. Let your focus gravitate towards what is true, what is honest, just, pure, and lovely. Cultivate thoughts that are of a good report, using virtue and praiseworthiness as your measures of quality.

However, it's not enough merely to replenish your strength. The key lies in maintaining it. Just as a well-nourished tree stands tall against the fiercest storms, so too must you feed your spirit to withstand life's tempests. Enrich your spiritual reservoir by drawing from the infinite wellspring of God's Word. Make it a daily practice to soak in His teachings, to immerse yourself in His promises.

Life's trials, as daunting as they may be, are not to be feared but utilized as our daily nourishment to strengthen our resolve. They are the anvil upon which our spirit is shaped, the crucible that tempers our faith. Therefore, let not your strength be defined by the absence of strife but by the grace with which you meet each difficulty. Draw from the Source of all strength, and no mountain shall seem too high, no path too daunting.

As you journey forward, remember this: strength does not lie solely in overcoming obstacles but in the courage to face them, in the faith to persist, and most importantly, in the wisdom to lean on God, the inexhaustible source of our strength.

Prayer

Lord, thank You for the boundless strength You have made available to me. You did not leave us powerless here on this earth, neither did You leave us alone to wander through this life without direction or empowerment. Thank You, Father, for equipping us with Your mighty Word and for giving us the measure of faith we need to enact Your will upon this earth. Now, Father, You know there are many times when my own strength fails and I feel as if I'm running on fumes. Yet, I'm encouraged because Your Word says You give power to the faint, and for those who have no might, You increase their strength. You said that those who wait upon You will renew their strength. This tells me that You are not surprised when my strength and my ability are not enough, when I require Your strength to make it through this life here on earth.

So, in accordance with Your Word, I ask You to give me strength. Help me to draw my strength from You so the demands of daily living cannot pull me down or wear me out. Let Your strength produce spiritual resilience, physical stamina, and mental sharpness in me. Help me resist the temptation to give in or give up. When my strength begins to waver, I pray that Your strength will take over. Help me draw strength from You so that I will not grow weary. You are my Source of energy and my Source of strength. In Your presence, I gain the strength I need to endure, the power I need to overcome, and the sustaining joy I need to conquer any challenge that may come my way. As I study and meditate on Your Word, I thank You that I find comfort and peace and that my strength is renewed.

In Jesus' name, amen.

Scriptures

He giveth power to the faint; and to them that have no might he increaseth strength.

—Isaiah 40:29

But they that wait upon the Lord shall renew their strength; they shall mount up with wings as eagles; they shall run, and not be weary; and they shall walk, and not faint.

—Isaiah 40:31

I have strength for all things in Christ Who empowers me [I am ready for anything and equal to anything through Him Who infuses inner strength into me; I am self-sufficient in Christ's sufficiency].

—Philippians 4:13 (AMP)

"The Lord is my strength and my shield; my heart trusts in him, and he helps me. My heart leaps for joy, and with my song I praise him."

—Psalm 28:7 (NIV)

"Finally, my brethren, be strong in the Lord, and in the power of his might."

—Ephesians 6:10 (KJV)

Thoughts

"Our strength is like the roots of the old oak tree, drawing from the deep well of living water that is Christ, giving us the resilience to stand strong amidst the strongest gales."

—D.L. Moody

"Lord, make me an instrument of your peace. Where there is hatred, let me sow love; where there is injury, pardon; where there is doubt, faith; where there is despair, hope; where there is darkness, light; where there is sadness, joy.

O, Divine Master, grant that I may not so much seek to be consoled as to console; to be understood as to understand; to be loved as to love; For it is in giving that we receive; it is in pardoning that we are pardoned; it is in dying that we are born again to eternal life."

—St Francis of Assisi

16

Peace

It seems like we are all constantly searching for more peace in our lives. Every day our peace is under constant attack. The flow of text messages and emails from friends, family, and people we don't even know; the daily grind of work and everyday living; and the challenges that life throws at us on a regular basis can stress us out to the point there is no peace in our lives.

But is peace just the lack of feeling stressed, tired, or anxious? Can it be gained by a quiet evening, reading a novel, or watching a favorite show on TV? Such moments may offer a temporary peace, that could better be described as a cease fire. That type of peace is obtained by disengaging from the world, and then it evaporates the moment we reconnect with the real world and its daily demands. Yet, there is a real peace, a supernatural peace that the world doesn't understand. It opens to you the simple joys of everyday life regardless of the chaos that may ensue around you. It's a divine peace strait from heaven and enjoyed by a simple choice of where you choose to look and who you are putting your trust in.

Peace does not equate to denial. It doesn't mean burying your head in the sand when the pressures of the day threaten to crush you. Peace is not a passive agreement between you and God, but an active state of being, accessible through your confident trust in Him. Knowing God's word and placing your trust in Him allows you to walk on the sunny side of life. You might not know what tomorrow holds or how to meet the day's demands, but you know the One who does. Indeed, problems arise, and temptations, fears, worries, and anxious thoughts will attempt to overtake you. When Jesus left this earth after being resurrected, He said, "Peace I leave with you; my peace I give unto you; not as the world giveth, give I unto you, let not your heart be troubled, let it be afraid" (John 14:27)

Its up to us not to let these daily issues and thoughts trouble us, but then the question is, How? Isaiah chapter 26, He said, "I will keep him in perfect peace, whose mind is stayed on me."

As you go throughout your day, if you notice an uptake in worries, anxiety, or even a crisis comes out of left field and knocks you off your feet, then take the opportunity to move your eyes from off of the wind and the waves of the storm and put them back on Jesus. Living this way allows you to savor an after-work book or movie in a way you never thought possible. No longer are you escaping from a world you'd rather not be part of to achieve a sense of peace and enjoyment, just enjoying a new moment in it.

Prayer

Lord, I thank You for giving me Your peace—the very same peace that Jesus operated in when He was on the earth, the same peace that caused Him to walk calmly through every kind of threat and problem. That same peace leads me and guides me, answering and deciding with finality all the questions that arise in my mind and my soul. I declare that Your peace acts as a state of being in which my soul, full of confidence in You, finds rest and contentment regardless of the situation or circumstances surrounding me. Your peace transcends human understanding, and I thank You for this wonderful gift of peace. Father, I ask for Your help to remain in Your peace and not allow my attention to falter or my trust to be pulled away from You.

Father, I ask that You would set a watch on my heart, that I would be alerted to anything that would come along in my day and tempt me to forsake my peace, exchanging it for a troubled mind. I ask for Your help to maintain Your peace and not to be distraught or frustrated when unexpected glitches or difficulties pop up in my life. Remind me to keep my eyes and thoughts fixed on You so that I may enter the place of rest and peace that can only be found in Your presence. Help me not to react badly or become agitated because of what other people say or do. Help me to keep my mind at peace and my heart steady when I am tempted to worry or become fearful because of the circumstances around me. Help me to have confident assurance in the fact that everything will work out just fine if I will keep calm and put my trust in You.

In Jesus' name, amen.

Scriptures

Peace I leave with you, my peace I give unto you: not as the world giveth, give I unto you. Let not your heart be troubled, neither let it be afraid.

—JOHN 14:27

Thou wilt keep him in perfect peace, whose mind is stayed on thee: because he trusteth in thee.

—ISAIAH 26:3

And let the peace (soul harmony which comes) from Christ rule (act as umpire continually) in your hearts [deciding and settling with finality all questions that arise in your minds, in that peaceful state] to which as [members of Christ's] one body you were also called [to live]. And be thankful (appreciative), [giving praise to God always].

—COLOSSIANS 3:15 (AMP)

And God's peace [shall be yours, that tranquil state of a soul assured of its salvation through Christ, and so fearing nothing from God and being content with its earthly lot of whatever sort that is, that peace] which transcends all understanding shall garrison *and* mount guard over your hearts and minds in Christ Jesus.

—PHILIPPIANS 4:7 (AMP)

Thoughts

....
....
....
....
....
....
....
....
....
....
....
....
....
....
....
....
....
....
....
....
....
....
....

"Let your door stand open to receive Him, unlock your soul to Him, offer Him a welcome in your mind, and then you will see the riches of simplicity, the treasures of peace, the joy of grace."

—St. Ambrose

"Courage doesn't always roar. Sometimes courage is the little voice at the end of the day that says I'll try again tomorrow."

—MARY ANNE RADMACHER

"Be calm and strong and patient. Meet failure and disappointment with courage. Rise superior to the trials of life and never give in to hopelessness or despair."

—DR WILLIAM OSLER

17

Courage

When most of us think of courage, we think about acts of heroism on the field of battle, a fireman running into a burning building to rescue a small child from certain death, or a complete stranger diving into a flood-swollen stream to save an elderly woman just before her car is engulfed by the rising waters.

The opportunity to respond courageously is not just reserved for extreme situations. Acts of courage are often much less flashy and dramatic, but no less significant. Courage is the audacity to speak up when you lack the perfect words, knowing that your voice has value even if it shakes. It's waking up at 5:00 a.m. every day to go to a job they dislike to provide for their family. Its the decision to get back up after a defeat. To strive for a dream that seems hopeless. Its smiling when you feel like crying, being a source of encouragement when you yourself feel discouraged. Courage is weaponized virtue. It's putting into action all the best that is within you regardless of what the outcome may be. Courage exercised in the heart of a child of God becomes a shield for the innocent, a voice for the voiceless, and a beacon of light in the darkness. It's the conviction that there are things in this life that's worth fighting for.

Your life is a precious gift, and it's worth every effort. Refuse to go quietly into the night or shirk back in fear when faced with an uncertain future. Instead, dare to step out in faith, to confront the shadows with Faith in God.

Courage is not just about fighting battles outside, it's about winning the battles within, against fear, against despair, against complacency. Life may be filled with unrecognized efforts, betrayed trusts, and underutilized passions, but it takes true courage to cast aside those disappointments and invest anyway. It takes courage to throw your whole self into your relationship with God, to be a pillar in your family, a blessing to your job, and a shinning example in your community. Every time you choose to fight, every time you choose to care, to hope, to love, and to persevere, you are being courageous. That's the beauty of courage - it grows stronger every time we dare to use it.

So how do you gain courage when the weight of the world seems too heavy to bear? Begin by remembering what you are fighting for and who stands alongside you in the battle. There are things in life worth every ounce of your strength, your time, your courage. Growing your relationship with your heavenly father, Building His kingdom, Obeying His commands, being an extension of His love to a dying and broken world, just to name a few.

Your daily opposition, whatever form it takes, is no match for the power of God. When you feel weak, recall this truth: God is not only a spectator of your struggle but an active participant in your battle. His strength becomes your strength; His courage becomes your courage. With God on your side, the impossible becomes possible, the unbearable becomes bearable.

He's right there with you in every step, in every challenge. His promise is unshakeable — He won't let you down and He won't ever leave you. He provides, guides, and when necessary, carries you through.

Remember to draw strength from His words. There are numerous instances in the Bible where God assures His people to be bold and courageous. One such instance is in the book of Joshua: "This is my command—be strong and courageous! Do not be afraid or discouraged. For the Lord your God is with you wherever you go" Joshua 1:9 (NLT).

Harness the word of God as a shield against fear and a sword against despair. Courage isn't about not feeling fear, but about stepping forward in spite of it, and with God by your side, you will never step alone.

Prayer

Lord, thank You for being with me, for never forsaking me, and for always being the stabilizing force in my life. I know that courageous living and boldly speaking Your Word does not require the absence of negative feelings or situations, but rather, they triumph over them. I ask for Your help to be bold and courageous in my life here on the earth. Rather than asking to never be put in a situation where I might be stretched or uncomfortable, I am asking for the inner strength to push past the fear and doubt and step out in faith, knowing that if I lack anything, You'll make up the difference. Help me not to match the demands of the moment to my own abilities and skill set, but to compare it to Your ability and skill sets. Teach me to see things as You do, to believe in myself as You believe in me.

Help me to face the uncertainties of this life with an undaunted spirit of courage and confidence: the courage to fight for what I believe in; the courage to be unshakeable in my faith; the courage to have the determination never to quit or give in when times are tough. Help me to continually remember that I can do all things through You, who gives me strength. Even though I may feel weak or fearful at times, I know that You are not. With You on my side, I can overcome anything. I draw my strength from my union with You. Help me to have complete confidence in Your ability in me and through me to face any problem and overcome any difficulty. Grant me boldness that I may face any situation with firmness of purpose and a strong resolve. Through You, I am more than a conqueror—I am a world overcomer.

In Jesus' name, amen.

Scriptures

Be strong and of a good courage, fear not, nor be afraid of them: for the Lord thy God, he it is that doth go with thee; he will not fail thee, nor forsake thee.

—DEUTERONOMY 31:6

This is my command—be strong and courageous! Do not be afraid or discouraged. For the Lord your God is with you wherever you go.

—JOSHUA 1:9 (NLT)

Be ye strong therefore, and let not your hands be weak: for your work shall be rewarded.

—2 CHRONICLES 15:7

Be on your guard; stand firm in the faith; be courageous; be strong.

—1 CORINTHIANS 16:13 (NIV)

"Wait on the LORD; be of good courage, and He shall strengthen your heart; Wait, I say, on the LORD!"

—PSALM 27:14 (NKJV)

David was greatly distressed, for the men spoke of stoning him because the souls of them all were bitterly grieved, each man for his sons and daughters. But David encouraged and strengthened himself in the Lord his God.

—1 SAMUEL 30:6 (AMPC)

Thoughts

"Courage is not having the strength to go on; it is going on when you don't have the strength."

—THEODORE ROOSEVELT

"Great faith is the product of great fights, great testimonies are the outcome of great tests, great triumphs can only come out of great trials, every stumbling block must become a stepping stone and every opposition must become an opportunity."

—SMITH WIGGLESWORTH

NOW FAITH is the assurance (the confirmation, the title deed) of the things [we] hope for, being the proof of things [we] do not see and the conviction of their reality [faith perceiving as real fact what is not revealed to the senses].

—HEBREWS 11:1 (AMP)

18

Faith

What is faith? This simple, yet profound question is often summarized by an eloquent definition from the Bible. It refers to faith as "The substance of things hoped for, the evidence of things not seen." A tad cryptic, isn't it? Let's unwrap it in today's vernacular. Essentially, faith serves as the steadfast foundation for our deepest aspirations and the convincing proof of an unseen, spiritual realm.

At its most basic level, faith is about trust, akin to the unflinching confidence we have in a sturdy chair or the ground we walk on to support us. Wherever you are standing or siting right now, has it occurred to you that ground or chair may not support you? Well, Can you imagine applying this same level of trust to God? Faith is the Foundation for bright and joyful expectation in our Good God, see the correlation? Most of the time when we pray, we don't really expect things to change, we just desire them too, and plead to God for them too. Faith expects them to because you are convinced of the sturdy and unfailing nature of God just like you are convinced of the sturdy nature of the ground beneath your feet. The reward for such trust brings us to the second part of the verse: evidence (or Proof) of things not seen (the spiritual realm). We see our situation change and miracles manifest.

The power of faith is transformative and essential. It is the key that unlocks the manifold blessings of God, the dynamic catalyst that sets the stage for miracles to unfold in our lives.

It's impossible to genuinely please God without Faith. So then then how do we increase our faith, or come to trust in God to such a level. The bible tells us that Faith comes by hearing and continuing to hear the Word of God. God is inseparable from his Word, as we read it, study it, pray it, talk about it, structure our life around it, meditate on it, and honor it as the final authority in our lives, then we foster a more intimate relationship with God. This communion fuels our faith, igniting it from a mere ember into a vibrant flame. The more we delve into His promises and understand who God is, what He has already done for us, and what He has pledged to do, the stronger our faith becomes.

You may hear stories of Amazing mountain moving, sea splitting, boat sinking, water walking faith, even in modern times as the blind see, the dead are raise, and the lame walk, and feel as though your faith is so small that you barely have enough faith to make it through the day. Don't be discouraged, God knows exactly where you are at, and like the prodigal son, will come running to meet you the moment you take a step towards him. Take your eyes off of others and put it back on God and His word.

Even in the most trying times, when you are at your weakest and your reservoir of faith feels empty, muster up the courage to say "Lord, I trust that your love for me is more significant than my doubts, my fears, and all my imperfections. I make the choice to meditate on your word instead of my situation and doubts." The simplest prayer, becomes a testament to our faith, expressing our conviction that He will come to our aid.

So begin your journey with God. You can really hear his voice and be all that you dream to be for His Kingdom, but it requires you to believe, and to act on that Belief. Have Faith in God.

Prayer

Lord, I thank You for giving me a measure of faith that I grow and foster for myself. Thank You for Your life-giving Word, which causes faith to come. Father, I know that faith pleases You, and that faith is not something the world understands or puts value upon. Father, if faith pleases You, I want to grow and mature the portion of faith You have given me as much as possible. I ask that You would send solid, faith-based teaching and teachers into my life. I ask that You would reveal to me how to apply this faith You have given in my everyday life and encourage me when my faith feels weak.

Help me not to buckle underneath the pain and problems that arise in this life. Help me not to roll over and accept bad reports as the final word. I ask that You would remind me what Your Word has said; help me remember which report I should believe: Yours or the world's. Faith is the victory that overcomes every test and trial that arises in this life—faith in You.

I ask that You would increase my awareness of You and Your work in my life. Help me to take time out of my day to pray so I can talk to You, and help me read Your Word so I can hear what You are saying to me. I ask that You would help me trust You more fully with all my obligations in life. Help me remember that You are always with me, so when things get tough, my faith in You will see me through whatever I face. Finally, Lord, I sincerely ask for Your patience with me as I learn to trust You wholly in every area of my life. Thank You, Lord, in Jesus' name, amen.

Scriptures

For [if we are] in Christ Jesus, neither circumcision nor uncir-
cumcision counts for anything, but only faith activated and
energized and expressed and working through love.

—GALATIANS 5:6 (AMP)

So then faith cometh by hearing, and hearing by the word of God.

—ROMANS 10:17

For we walk by faith, not by sight.

—2 CORINTHIANS 5:7

For whatsoever is born of God overcometh the world: and this is
the victory that overcometh the world, even our faith.

—1 JOHN 5:4

Now faith is the assurance (the confirmation, the title deed) of
the things [we] hope for, being the proof of things [we] do not
see and the conviction of their reality [faith perceiving as real
fact what is not revealed to the senses]. For by [faith—trust
and holy fervor born of faith] the men of old had divine testimony borne to them and obtained a good report. By faith we
understand that the worlds [during the successive ages] were
framed (fashioned, put in order, and equipped for their intended
purpose) by the word of God, so that what we see was not made
out of things which are visible.

—HEBREWS 11:1-3 (AMPC)

Thoughts

"Faith never knows where it is being led, but it loves and knows the One who is leading."

—OSWALD CHAMBERS

He cares for you,
and knows your troubles too
so cast each one upon Him
and watch what He will do.

He cares for you,
knows each hair on your head
and all of His little sparrows
God has always fed.

He cares for you,
let not anxiety be your guide
humble yourself before Him
and He'll never leave your side.

He cares for you,
are you not just as splendid
as all the lilies in the field
to which He has always tended.

He cares for you,
and carries your burdens too
so, submit your life to Him
and trust in what He can do!

—Deborah Ann Belka

19

Casting My Cares

These are crazy times. Wars breaking out up around the war. World's political environment is unstable, with wars and threats of wars producing daily unrest. The economy is in a constant state of flux and the national debt is out of control. New disease threats like covid, Ebola, and superbugs that are resistant to all known antibiotics are popping up at an unprecedented rate. No matter who is in the White House, or what political party has control of Congress, nothing seems to get done. We also find ourselves vulnerable to unconventional enemies like identity theft and cyber-terrorism.

There are proclamations being made in the media and parades in the streets that just a few years ago could only be heard as whispers in a dark alley. The truth has become taboo, disagreements grounds for cancelation, and family values an antiquated ideal. With the moral compass of the world spiraling down out of control, and evil on the prowl, it begs the question: how can we walk confidently through such instability?

Add to that the personal challenges of everyday, It is easy to become overwhelmed by a sense of hopelessness. If we are not careful, we can let the cares of this life make us want to crawl into a hole and hide.

There is good news for you today, Jesus is not surprised by anything that is going on in your life or the world. Jesus assured us that we would encounter trials and tribulations in this life, but he also urged us to remain resilient and steadfast, free from worry, for He has overcome the world and is always with us, guiding and protecting us. He acknowledged that the path of righteousness is often beset with challenges, yet he promised to deliver us from them all. The scriptures remind us to entrust all our anxieties, worries, and fears to Him, for He deeply cares for us and doesn't wish for us to be encumbered by the hardships of this world.

Jesus extends an open invitation, "Come to me, all you who are weary and burdened, and I will give you rest" Matthew 11:28 (NIV). He promises relief, a release from our burdens, and refreshment for our souls.

So how do we not become overwhelmed and unsteady? How can we live with joy, sleep with peace, and walk with confidence when all this turmoil threating to invade our homes: By believing the words of Jesus and casting our cares on him. We know what the world does not, we gather our strength and stability from an endless well of Christ's love and power. This means that we and our families will not be victims of a sin ridden environment, but overcomers and conquerors of it even as Christ was and is.

Today, surrender all your worries to Jesus and find rest in His grace. Allow His divine peace to calm your heart amid the turmoil of this world. For in Him, we find the courage to navigate life's uncertainties, fortified by a faith that is both enduring and unshakable.

Prayer

Lord, You said in Your Word to cast the whole of my cares, all my anxieties, all my worries, all my concerns, once and for all, onto You, because You care for me affectionately and You look after me watchfully. Thank You for being so attentive to me, for watching over me, and for caring for me so deeply. Knowing how big You are, and how small my problems are by comparison, makes me feel so special. I know that even the smallest problems I experience don't escape Your notice and, in fact, You want to carry them for me.

I recall You have also said in Your Word that although we will have various problems in this world, You will deliver us from them all. You said that I should cast my cares on You and that You would sustain me, not letting me be shaken. Father, I thank You for Your promises and Your love, which has so evidently been put on display for my sake.

Father, I would like to take this opportunity to cast all my cares, anxieties, worries, and concerns onto You. I ask that You would remind me of all these promises daily, so I would not take on the weight of any problems as burdens in my thought life. No matter the size of the problem—big or small—I know You want me to be free from all care and worry. Because of this, I ask You to help me grow more reliant on You, not fretting over the things that happen in my life. Remind me of the truth of my situation—that no amount of worry will help me, my friends, or my family. Only You can help. Lord, I ask that You take these cares that are weighing on my mind so that I may be free to live this life full of joy and peace.

In Jesus' name, amen.

Scriptures

Casting the whole of your care, all your anxieties, all your worries, all your concerns, once and for all on Him, for He cares for you affectionately and cares about you watchfully.

—1 PETER 5:7 (AMP)

Come unto me, all ye that labour and are heavy laden, and I will give you rest.

—MATTHEW 11:28

Cast your cares on the LORD and he will sustain you; he will never let the righteous be shaken.

—PSALMS 55:22 (NIV)

The righteous person may have many troubles, but the Lord delivers him from them all.

—PSALM 34:19 (NIV)

The LORD is good, a refuge in times of trouble. He cares for those who trust in him.

NAHUM 1:7 (NIV)

You will keep in perfect peace those whose minds are steadfast, because they trust in you. Trust in the LORD forever, for the LORD, the LORD himself, is the Rock eternal.

ISAIAH 26:3-4 (NIV)

Thoughts

"Every evening, I turn my worries over to God. He's going to be up all night anyway."

—MARY C. CROWLEY

"Bad things do happen: how I respond to them defines my character and the quality of my life. I can choose to sit in perpetual sadness, immobilized by the gravity of my loss, or I can choose to rise from the pain and treasure the most precious gift I have— life itself."

—Walter Anderson

When written in Chinese, the word 'crisis' is composed of two characters. One represents danger and the other represents opportunity.

Danger   Opportunity

20

Facing a Crisis

Experiencing a crisis can be unexpected and sudden, but is not a unique experience to the human condition. In fact, though we may wish it were different, crisis is a normal part of life, even for us as believers. It could manifest as a major illness, financial ruin, an unexpected divorce, or the death of a loved one. While Crisis situations are unsettling, and often tragic, they don't have to destroy you.

When the crisis manifests itself, it becomes the easiest thing in the world to blame yourself, others or God. It becomes easy to allow the whirlwind of emotions to overwhelm and overtake you. It seems natural to pull the covers over your head, shut out the world, and wall yourself off to any semblance of hope or joy. Then, there burns a question in our mind that seems inescapable: Why? But regardless of how much soul-searching, complaining, or frustration we undergo for the answer to this question, we are faced with the reality that our circumstances remain the same. There will be a time to ask the Lord for guidance on how to avoid or prepare for such things is the future, but, in moments of crisis, it's time to quiet all other questions and ask, "What do I need to do now?"

When your backed into a corner, with fear and grief tag teaming your demise, there is only two responses left to you: To Give Up or To Fight.

Your response will determine weather this crisis becomes a devastating event that becomes the focal point of your life, or a tragedy that Gods grace was sufficient enough to see you through. Determining to stay on God's side no matter what, choosing to focus on what the bible says about your situation, and choosing to press on in faith despite all of the emotions and thoughts trying to destroy you is fighting the fight of faith in your crisis. It is not bad to feel grief, doubt, and despair when tragedy strikes, but it is deadly to let these emotions monopolize your thought life and define who you are, now, after the crisis has struck. There is a metamorphosis that happens in extreme crisis. There is no stopping it. You will come out of the other side different. If you loose someone you love, you'll go through that metamorphosis, but rather that metamorphosis is brought on by a grief and despair or brought on by Christ's love and grace is determined by where you put your focus. It is your choice rather you will define yourself as a casualty of tragedy or an overcomer. Mercy is enough.

Embracing this mindset of resilience and faith is empowering. Every crisis is also an opportunity – a chance to grow stronger, to deepen our faith, and to discover aspects of ourselves and God that we may not have known before. While we can't control the crises that come our way, we can control our response. A sense of perspective, combined with unwavering faith, can make all the difference. It's in the midst of our most trying moments that our character is truly tested and defined. By placing our hardships in God's hands, we're not just relinquishing control but aligning ourselves with a higher purpose and power. It's a reminder that even in our weakest moments, we're never truly alone. God's enduring presence serves as a beacon of hope, guiding us through the storms and into a brighter tomorrow.

Prayer

Lord, I am so thankful there is no situation that catches You by surprise. It encourages me to know that though life may present unexpected and sudden issues that catch me off guard, You are never unprepared; You always stand ready with the grace and wisdom I need to help me through any situation. Father, I realize that crisis is a normal part of life, but I also know that despair, confusion, and feeling overwhelmed don't have to be. I know that with each crisis also comes the ability and opportunity to conquer and overcome. So, Father, I ask for Your help to be more than a conqueror and an overcomer in this life.

Father, help me to be patient and trusting when I face the difficulties in my life. Help me not to become fearful, anxious, or overwhelmed when I find myself in a crisis. Help me not to react in confusion, worry, or desperation. Show me how to keep a good attitude and a cheerful heart no matter what I am facing. Help me to keep my mind fixed on You—knowing that You will see me through. Give me wisdom and insight concerning any decisions I need to make or any actions I need to take. Thank You for giving me the courage, strength, and fortitude not to give up or give in, but to keep trusting You until this crisis is resolved.

Finally, I ask You, Lord, for resilience. Help me to be like a battle-tested soldier: firm and resolute in times of crisis. I ask that I would be a help to others, that You would help my light to shine even brighter when things are not going well for me. Help me trust in You for rescue and salvation, so that I may be used by You in turn to help rescue others. Help me to trust in You to anchor me when all that is around me seems to be on shifting sand. I want to be a stabilizing force in the lives of others and teach them of the solid foundation that is Your Word. Thank You, Lord, for hearing and answering my prayer.

In Jesus' name, amen.

Scriptures

Is anyone crying for help? GOD is listening, ready to rescue you. If your heart is broken, you'll find GOD right there; if you're kicked in the gut, he'll help you catch your breath. Disciples so often get into trouble; still, GOD is there every time.

—PSALM 34:17-19 (MSG)

..I have learned in any and all circumstances the secret of facing every situation, whether well-fed or going hungry, having a sufficiency *and* enough to spare or going without *and* being in want. I have strength for all things in Christ Who empowers me [I am ready for anything and equal to anything through Him Who infuses inner strength into me; I am self-sufficient in Christ's sufficiency].

—PHILIPPIANS 4:12B-13 (AMP)

Because of the Lord's great love we are not consumed, for his compassions never fail. They are new every morning; great is your faithfulness.

—LAMENTATIONS 3:22-23 (NIV)

When you go through deep waters, I will be with you. When you go through rivers of difficulty, you will not drown. When you walk through the fire of oppression, you will not be burned up; the flames will not consume you.

—ISAIAH 43:2 (NLT)

Thoughts

"God, who foresaw your tribulation, has specially armed you to go through it, not without pain but without stain."

—C.S. Lewis

"We should be too big to take
offense and too noble to give it."

—ABRAHAM LINCOLN

"As I walked out the door toward the gate
that would lead to my freedom I knew if I
didn't leave my bitterness and hatred behind I
would still be in prison."

—NELSON MANDELA
(after 27 years of wrongful imprisonment)

21

Dealing with Offense

Offense is the unwelcome guest at the dinner table, the shadow lurking in the corners of our relationships—constantly seeking avenues to infiltrate our peace. An unkind word, a dismissive look, or a thoughtless action, offense waits in the ordinary, ready to ambush us with resentment and bitterness.

However, a powerful choice lies within our hands—the choice not to be offended. Embracing this choice means cultivating a mindset anchored in love and fortified by the wisdom of God's Word. It allows us to discern the motives behind the words or actions that seem hurtful, enabling us to respond with grace and understanding.

When offense knocks at the door of our hearts, we can choose to reflect rather than react. Is the person who delivered the hurtful words undergoing pain themselves? Are their words a mirror of their own struggles and not necessarily a reflection of our shortcomings? We can take a moment to sift through the words, separating the chaff from the grain, determining whether there's any merit to the offense or if it's merely a manifestation of another's hurt.

If the words carry weight, let us use them as tools for growth, aligning ourselves more closely with God's purpose for our lives. If they are baseless, we allow them to fall away, leaving our peace and joy unscathed. Grounding our identities in the solid rock of God's Word enables us to withstand the tempests of hurtful words and actions. We replace the whispers of offense with the loving and affirming words of our Father, ensuring that our thoughts are rooted in love and truth.

Finally, Forgiveness is the armor that guards our hearts against offense. It's the antidote for the poison of bitterness inflicted by harsh words and thoughtless actions. As we adorn ourselves with forgiveness, we embody God's love, letting go of the need for earthly justice and revenge.

In choosing not to be offended, we walk through life with uplifted with joy, guided by peace, and grounded in love and grace. We nurture relationships infused with grace and understanding, cultivating an environment where love can flourish. Our lives become testimonies of God's transformative power, reflecting His boundless love and wisdom in our interactions with others. So, let us choose love over offense, allowing our actions to relay all of the love, grace, and forgiveness we have received from God to all of those we come in contact with.

Prayer

Lord, I thank You for being the Source of my identity. When others comment unfavorably on my appearance, You tell me I am fearfully and wonderfully made. When others ignore me, You number the hairs on my head. When others treat me as worthless, You put my worth and Your love for me on display for all to see—because You sent Your own Son to die for my sake. When others mock me and belittle me, You build me up, reminding me that I have a spirit of power, and love, and a sound mind. When other people overlook my contributions, I know You take special note when I do even the smallest act in Your name, like giving a drink of water to someone who is thirty, for the sake of Your Kingdom. Father, I know that my heart is at its safest in Your arms, and that my mental health and confidence are at their peak when I am trusting in and obeying You. So, Father, I ask that You would remind me of who I am to You whenever I'm tempted to be offended by what other people think of or say about me.

Father, I ask that You would grant me the ability to see people the way You see them. You love me so unconditionally, regardless of my many offenses against You. Help me to draw on that love so I can show that same love to all those around me. I ask that You would help me stay calm and in control of my emotions any time an opportunity for offense may come my way. Help me remember to take a deep breath when people are rude to me, realizing that You are my Source and I do not need to take offense. I ask that You would remove any bitterness or grudges that I am holding on to in my heart. I know that only hurts me, so please give me the strength to forgive and the peace to forget. Thank You, Lord, for helping me be free to enjoy the abundant life You have provided for me.

In Jesus' name, amen.

Scriptures

The one who forgives an offense seeks love, but whoever repeats a matter separates close friends.

—PROVERBS 17:9 (NET)

Understand [this], my beloved brethren. Let every man be quick to hear [a ready listener], slow to speak, slow to take offense and to get angry.

—JAMES 1:19 (AMP)

Above all things have intense and unfailing love for one another, for love covers a multitude of sins [forgives and disregards the offenses of others].

—1 PETER 4:8 (AMP)

Good sense makes one slow to anger, and it is his glory to overlook an offense.

—PROVERBS 19:11 (ESV)

And blessed is the one who is not offended by me.

—LUKE 7:23 (ESV)

"Make allowance for each other's faults, and forgive anyone who offends you. Remember, the Lord forgave you, so you must forgive others."

—COLOSSIANS 3:13 (NLT)

Thoughts

"I will permit no man to narrow and degrade my soul by making me hate him."

—Booker T. Washington

To forgive is to set a prisoner free
and discover the prisoner was you.

—Lewis B. Smedes

"O Lord, remember not only the men and
women of good will, but also those of ill will.
But do not remember all of the suffering they
have inflicted upon us, instead remember the
fruits we have borne because of this suffering—
our fellowship, our loyalty to one another,
our humility, our courage, our generosity, the
greatness of heart that has grown from this
trouble. When our persecutors come to be
judged by you, let all of these fruits that we have
borne be their forgiveness."

—(Found in the clothing of a dead child
at Ravensbruck concentration camp.)

22

Forgiveness

Forgiveness is the cornerstone of the Christian experience. Jesus offers unequivocal forgiveness to everyone who believes in Him and receives Him as Lord. No matter what you have done, no matter how disgraceful your deeds or actions, there is complete and total forgiveness available to you if you would only ask for it. Jesus Loves you, He is not ashamed of you, and extends his hand of forgiveness to all who asks for it. It's the first and greatest miracle of Christianity. Our finite mind can hardly grasp the wonder, scope, and beauty of the Lord's forgiveness. You can't earn it; you don't deserve it. It's God's gift to you.

Now it's your turn. The Bible says we should forgive others just like Christ has forgiven us. Maybe you are harboring unforgiveness in your heart towards someone. It may be because of the betrayal of a close friend, a failed marriage, or a boss that passed you over for a well-deserved promotion. Maybe it's the result of a more serious violation like physical, verbal, or sexual abuse. Whatever the case, with God's Help you can forgive them.

Forgiveness is a process, one that starts with the choice to forgive by faith, even if the offender is unapologetic, and it is followed up with a daily choice to replace all thoughts of betrayal and bitterness with thoughts of God's Love and mercy. As you undergo this heart process, You'll begin to enjoy a freedom and a peace that passes understanding. This process may not happen overnight, but as time passes your heart will begin to mend, and the power, that the offender's actions have to affect you negatively, will gradually diminish.

And now, the toughest of all—you need to forgive *yourself*. Maybe it's your own actions that eat away at you daily, keeping you trapped in a prison of regret. God forgives you, and now you need to forgive yourself and move into the bright and wonderful future that God has destined for you. God wants you to experience the beauty of forgiveness in every area of your life. So, even if you are ready to throw in the towel on yourself, even if years and decades have come and gone and you still are struggling with the same things, you still haven't even begun to scratch the surface of God's love, grace, and patience. You may not feel it, but with what God did by sacrificing His son to pay the price of your sins, He has already put on display for all to see your immeasurable worth to Him. Who are we to argue? Who are we to tell Him He got it wrong with us? Who are we to supersede His judgment of grace concerning us with our own judgment of condemnation? We have no course of action left to us but to forgive ourselves and others as God has forgiven us, and in so doing, grow confident in the power of the price paid for our forgiveness, to approach our heavenly Father boldly, as one who belongs, and receive the help and the hope we need.

Prayer

Lord, I thank You for the awesome gift of Your forgiveness and Your unconditional love. You said in Your Word to approach Your throne of grace boldly so that I may receive mercy and find grace to help me in my time of need. Father, I take note that You request my boldness when I come to Your throne of grace to get help and receive mercy; without boldness, it is wrong for me to approach Your throne—and yet, I desire Your mercy and forgiveness. Help me to be bold in receiving this forgiveness from You, knowing that You are love and You have already paid the price so that sin and condemnation doesn't destroy me from the inside out. I ask that the relationship I have with You would not be based on a constant cycle of sinfulness and shame, but that it would be one of confident repentance, even when I may sin, for I know who I am to you and that I am worthy because of what Jesus did on the cross.

Father, I ask that You would also help me to be bold in my forgiveness of others. Because I have been forgiven of so much, help me to be quick to forgive others. I pray for those who have hurt me in any way. I forgive them for anything they have done. I will not hate them, despise them, or desire that they suffer retribution for their actions against me. I ask You to forgive them, as well. I pray that You would reach out to them and minister Your loving-kindness to them. I release them from any offense that is in my heart. I will not gossip about them, ridicule them, or slander their character with others.

Finally, Lord, I ask You to help me forgive myself for my own failures, mistakes, and shortcomings. Help me to receive Your forgiveness so I can put the past behind me and move forward without guilt and condemnation, fulfilling the destiny You have for me.

In Jesus' name, amen.

Scriptures

Even if we feel guilty, God is greater than our feelings, and he knows everything. Dear friends, if we don't feel guilty, we can come to God with bold confidence.

—1 JOHN 3:20-21 (NLT)

He canceled the record of the charges against us and took it away by nailing it to the cross.

—COLOSSIANS 2:14 (NLT)

And be ye kind one to another, tenderhearted, forgiving one another, even as God for Christ's sake hath forgiven you.

—EPHESIANS 4:32

"Then Peter came to Jesus and asked, 'Lord, how many times shall I forgive my brother or sister who sins against me? Up to seven times?' Jesus answered, 'I tell you, not seven times, but seventy-seven times.'"

—MATTHEW 18:21-22 (NIV)

"Get rid of all bitterness, rage and anger, brawling and slander, along with every form of malice. Be kind and compassionate to one another, forgiving each other, just as in Christ God forgave you."

—EPHESIANS 4:31-32 (NIV)

"He has removed our sins as far from us as the east is from the west."

—PSALM 103:12 (NLT)

Thoughts

"Everyone thinks forgiveness is a lovely idea until he has something to forgive."

—C.S. Lewis:

"Joy is the infallible sign of the presence of God."

—Pierre Teilhard de Chardin

"Joy is distinctly a Christian word and a Christian thing. It is the reverse of happiness. Happiness is the result of what happens of an agreeable sort. Joy has its springs deep down inside. And that spring never runs dry, no matter what happens.

—S.D. Gordon

23

Joy

Everyone desires happiness. Everyone is looking for "it". They want to wake up every morning with a smile on their face, a song in their heart, and doing something meaningful and fun. This desire is a perfectly healthy one, but how most go about achieving it leaves them anything but happy. This is because what we are all really searching for is Joy.

Often we use the words "joy" and "happiness" interchangeably, but really there is a significant difference. Happiness is a product of our circumstances, but joy, on the other hand, comes from within. Happiness is a result of what happens to us. Joy is a result of what happens in us.

Often, people approach the Bible and their relationship with God with the expectation of external life changes, overlooking the truth:

It is not our situation in life that God changes. He changes us.

As we grow closer to God, valuing His ways and His Word, and cherishing the time spent in His presence, our focus shifts. Our minds and hearts are directed towards Him, leading to a transformation from the inside out. We begin to understand His immense love for us, our identity in Him, the blessings we possess through Him, and the potential we have in partnership with Him. It is this internal metamorphosis that then radiates outward, altering our life's trajectory. The happiness, purpose, and inner strength that everyone so desperately works their whole life to get is not difficult to acquire, it's a free gift that comes through our fellowship with God.

God assures us in His Word that being in His presence brings fullness of joy, a joy that becomes our strength. Embrace this joy, especially when facing life's trials, knowing that God will care for you. Instead of casting it away in tough times, let it be the stabilizing force that guides you and others through turbulence. Every day is a divine gift, so instead of yielding to complaints and shifting focus away from God onto our circumstances, we should rejoice and be glad, not in the problems but in His companionship. This practice of constant gratitude and joy, fostered through our growing relationship with God, lifts us above the ebb and flow of life's challenges.

Purpose in your heart to grow close to him and you will come to know that Joy is not a fleeting emotion but a deep-seated state of being. It transcends the temporary ups and downs of life, anchoring you in a sense of peace and contentment that is independent of external circumstances. This divine joy is a wellspring of hope and resilience that empowers you to navigate life's challenges with grace and fortitude. You'll begin to see that as your relationship with God grows, His joy begins permeating every aspect of our lives, transforming your perspective and enabling you to see the beauty and blessings in even the most mundane moments.

Prayer

Lord, I thank You for the wonderful gift of life! It is so amazing to be alive, to know You, to be Your child, to serve You, and to serve others in Your name. I know, Father, that the joy of the Lord is my strength. Whenever I feel as if life is unbearable, that the task at hand is too enormous for me to handle, please remind me to redirect my attention onto You so that I may rejoice in the midst of whatever test or trial I find myself. I know that true joy comes from You, and I want to live every day experiencing the fullness of Your joy and peace. I know that negative feelings, problems, challenges, and even attacks from the enemy will come in this life, but I also know that focusing on Your joy and peace is a choice. Help me to make that choice daily. Help me to rejoice no matter what I see, feel, or hear—not for the problems, not for the issues, but for the greater One who lives within me and helps me to overcome them. Father, help me to navigate my own downfalls with grace, allowing me to learn from them but not meditating on them and letting them steal my joy.

The Bible tells us that this is the day the Lord has made; we will rejoice and be glad in it (see Psalm 118:24). I can rejoice because I know You are with me. I know that You have made this day, that You know everything that is going to transpire in this day, and that You are right here beside me, ready to help me in every area if I only turn to You and ask for Your assistance. So, Father, I ask You for Your help—not to have a life in which I am barely making it each day, but to refine my perspective so that I go to bed and wake up each day with a smile on my face because You are with me, no matter what happens. I ask for Your help to walk in faith and experience Your joy and peace daily. Thank You for Your presence in my life.

In Jesus' name, amen.

Scriptures

"Strengthened with all might, according to his glorious power, unto all patience and longsuffering with joyfulness;

—COLOSSIANS 1:11

Now the God of hope fill you with all joy and peace in believing, that ye may abound in hope, through the power of the Holy Ghost.

—ROMANS 15:13

"......And be not grieved *and* depressed, for the joy of the Lord is your strength *and* stronghold."

—NEHEMIAH 8:10B (AMP)

My brothers and sisters, think of the various tests you encounter as occasions for joy. After all, you know that the testing of your faith produces endurance.

—JAMES 1:2-3 (CEB)

"Rejoice in the Lord always; again I will say, rejoice!"

—PHILIPPIANS 4:4 (NASB)

"You have turned my mourning into joyful dancing. You have taken away my clothes of mourning and clothed me with joy."

—PSALM 30:11 (NLT)

Thoughts

"Joy is the holy fire that keeps our purpose warm and our intelligence aglow."

—Helen Keller

There is a great darkness that doesn't wait for night,

A cold, empty void that hides the light.

It's the end to every beginning,

Feels as if your enemy is winning.

This cancer of the earth,

inescapable since birth.

We were not made for death,

To feel the pain of love's last breath,

The sin that brought loss to our homes,

Has been forgiven but its child still roams,

With its claws sharp but its sting removed,

The pain cuts deep but its poison subdued,

You have a daddy above,

The purest light named Love,

Ready to pierce the void,

So you won't be destroyed

Lean on him and the pain will slowly fade,

As the darkness turns to shade,

And the hope of tomorrow,

Begins to lessen yesterday's sorrow.

—JAKE PROVANCE

24

Loss

One thing that is universal to the human experience is loss. It's a sobering truth that while we are on this earth there is a beginning and an end to everything. Loss strikes in many different ways—a job, a relationship, the life of a loved one, your influence, your purpose, or simply your ability to do what you once could. Knowing that loss is an inevitable event we all must experience, it's so critical that we learn how to navigate all the pain, confusion, and frustration that occurs when we lose something or someone. Dealing with loss is a process, and it's OK to have feelings of grief, hurt, and confusion, but when you dwell on the pain of loss for too long it can monopolize your life and hinder your ability to heal.

When we experience loss, an emptiness is created that is proportional to how significant the thing was to us that we lost. Too often we try to fill the emptiness with the wrong stuff. We'll fill it up with distractions, thinking that the pain will go away if we don't think about it, but we end up only making our suffering longer. We may turn to seemingly harmless activities like immersing ourselves in online games, binge-watching TV shows, or even embarking on extended trips. While these activities offer a temporary respite, a momentary detachment from the weight of our emotions, they are not solutions. They serve as distractions, pauses in the relentless narrative of our grief. It's perfectly acceptable, and even necessary, to allow ourselves these breaks, these moments of lightness where we can breathe and find enjoyment amidst the turmoil. However, we must be cautious not to let these interludes become our primary way of coping. They should not be an escape from our feelings, but rather a gentle space where we can momentarily rest before returning to the crucial task of processing our emotions. In recognizing and honoring our need for these moments of reprieve, we can better navigate the balance between taking care of ourselves and confronting the realities of our loss. We may try to medicate our emptiness with drugs or alcohol, but we end up making the hole in our lives bigger by the self-destructive nature of substance abuse.

We could try to fill the emptiness with revenge and hatred, blaming others for its existence in the first place. The problem with these methods of dealing with loss is that we are running away from our hurt instead of running to God with our hurt. As you hope in God, you don't have to know how you will make it through, just know that you will—that sometime, somehow, everything will be OK because God is with you.

As you lean on God, the emptiness will begin to fade as God's life, love, and light takes its place.

The loss we feel in our hearts no longer has to monopolize every moment, nor does it have to act as a debilitating weight dragging behind us wherever we go. With God's Grace and unending love, and through the passage of time, we are guided towards a path of not just enduring our losses but growing from them, finding in our scars not just evidence of past pain, but also of present healing and future hope.

Prayer

Lord, I thank You for the ability to come to You with whatever I am facing. I thank You that when I feel at my lowest, when the pain of life is at its greatest intensity, I can run to You and receive the comfort and help I so desperately need. When I have lost someone I love, as I am experiencing the sorrow and grief that comes with that experience, I know You know how I feel. You lost Your most beloved Son—all for the sake of gaining me and my brothers and sisters in Christ. I can now relate to the pain You must have felt in that moment. And yet, Father, I know I don't grieve as the world grieves. I know there is still hope and happiness in my future. I know there is joy and new life still waiting for me. Yet the pain of loss blinds me from experiencing it at this time. Father, I ask You for Your tender love and mercy to help me get up and walk again, to see this life as You see it, and to experience the positive side of life on this earth again. Help me to navigate these complex emotions, and shed a light on what is true and good. Show me what is toxic for me to think and meditate on, and what is healthy to for me to process and to communicate.

I ask for Your wisdom, strength, and encouragement, and I ask that You would bring people—Your people, who have a shared understanding of loss—across my path to help me walk the life of faith after this tragedy. Lord, I ask You to heal my heart and to fill the gaps of my life left by loss with the hope that is found in You. You are more than enough for every need and every void that I am experiencing. Thank You, Lord, for Your help.

In Jesus' name, amen.

Scriptures

The Lord is close to the brokenhearted; he rescues those whose spirits are crushed.

—PSALM 34:18 (NLT)

He heals the brokenhearted and binds up their wounds [curing their pains and their sorrows].

—PSALM 147:3 (AMP)

Do not let your hearts be troubled (distressed, agitated). You believe in and adhere to and trust in and rely on God; believe in and adhere to and trust in and rely also on Me.

—JOHN 14:1 (AMP)

God will wipe away every tear from their eyes; and death shall be no more, neither shall there be anguish (sorrow and mourning) nor grief nor pain any more, for the old conditions and the former order of things have passed away.

—REVELATION 21:4 (AMP)

"And now, dear brothers and sisters, we want you to know what will happen to the believers who have died so you will not grieve like people who have no hope. For since we believe that Jesus died and was raised to life again, we also believe that when Jesus returns, God will bring back with him the believers who have died. We tell you this directly from the Lord: We who are still living when the Lord returns will not meet him ahead of those who have died. For the Lord himself will come down from heaven with a commanding shout, with the voice of the archangel, and with the trumpet call of God. First, the believers who have died will rise from their graves. Then, together with them, we who are still alive and remain on the earth will be caught up in the clouds to meet the Lord in the air. Then we will be with the Lord forever."

—1 THESSALONIANS 4:13-17 (NLT)

Thoughts

"O death, where is your victory? O death, where is your sting?"

—1 CORINTHIANS 15:55 ESV

Don't Quit
by John Greenleaf Whittier

When things go wrong as they sometimes will,
When the road you're trudging seems all up hill,
When the funds are low and the debts are high
And you want to smile, but you have to sigh,
When care is pressing you down a bit,
Rest if you must, but don't you quit.
Life is strange with its twists and turns
As every one of us sometimes learns
And many a failure comes about
When he might have won had he stuck it out;
Don't give up though the pace seems slow—
You may succeed with another blow.
Success is failure turned inside out—
The silver tint of the clouds of doubt,
And you never can tell just how close you are,
It may be near when it seems so far;
So stick to the fight when you're hardest hit—
It's when things seem worst that you must not quit.

25

Don't Quit

"Nobody may understand why you are struggling today or why thoughts of quitting linger in your mind. Perhaps the idea of quitting is just fleeting, or perhaps it has grown to the point where you feel at the end of your rope, having lost all hope. Life's challenges can bring anyone to their knees. It could be a life-altering event, such as the loss of a loved one, a life-threatening illness, a divorce, or impending financial ruin. Maybe it's the betrayal of a close friend or coworker, or perhaps it's your own actions—deceit and selfishness—that have alienated you from your loved ones. It might be negligence that caused misfortune and pain to those you cherish most, an addiction you cannot conquer, or repeated failures that have shattered your self-confidence, leaving you in a morass of discouragement and despair.

Regardless of the cause, there is still hope if you don't quit. That hope is Christ, who can lift you from your troubles if you allow Him. Crises, whether we like it or not, are a normal part of life in this world. Life is replete with ups and downs, joys and sorrows, victories and defeats, and grand accomplishments alongside heart-wrenching setbacks. Everything may seem perfect one day, only for the bottom to fall out the next. Being a Christian doesn't exempt us from these trials, but it does provide hope and stability to endure, Strength and Joy to Overcome, and faith to Conquer all.

Life on earth is ever-changing, and nothing seems stable or certain, but one thing is constant: Jesus. His love for you is unchanging. You might feel distant from God, as if your prayers go unheard, but nothing could be further from the truth. No mistake you've made can overshadow what Jesus did for you. God's grace and mercy continually overcome the sins of His children. All that is required is to ask for His help. With God's assistance, you can see light at the end of the tunnel and make it through. No matter the depth of your pit or the magnitude of your sins, His love is greater.

You may face what seems an insurmountable mountain, but God specializes in the impossible. There is a path to victory, a way out of despair, and hope for a brighter future. With God's help, you will overcome whatever challenge you face.

Don't quit. All is not lost; hope remains. The night won't overpower you, nor will darkness claim you. Your past doesn't define your future. You haven't run out of options. Don't quit. Stopping now is the only certain way to fail. The only way this becomes the end of your story, rather than just a chapter, is by quitting.

You are not powerless. There is untapped strength within you, a dormant force awaiting awakening. You are not alone! There's a peace that surpasses all understanding available to you, and a hope to fix your eyes upon. There's love that exceeds your highest dreams, and fears to be conquered. But you must not quit.

This isn't just a lofty dream; it's God's desire for you. You've tried life your way; now, it's time to try God's way. Cry out to Him, and He will respond. Through His Spirit and Word, you'll find the help, answers, courage, and strength to persevere and conquer even in the toughest circumstances.

Prayer

Father, I thank You for Your written Word, and that the Bible is actually filled with the words You are speaking to me. I thank You that You have declared in Your Word that You always cause me to triumph in Christ. You give me the victory through Him, and I am more than a conqueror because of Jesus. You said that in You, I can have perfect peace and confidence in this life. Although in this world I will have tribulation and trials, distress and frustration, I should be of good cheer and take courage, be confident, certain, and undaunted because You have overcome this world. You have deprived it of its power to harm me, conquering it for me. Thank You, Lord, that I am alive, that You have kept me safe, that You have delivered me from so many terrible situations. You have made a way for me when there was no way. Thank You, Lord.

Now, Father, I ask that You would remind me of all the times when You've delivered me when I was tempted to doubt. When I'm hardest hit by the troubles and problems of this world, help me to stay united with You. I ask for peace, clarity of mind, strength, and joy to make it through and continue to hope for the future. You have been, You are, and You always will be by my side, and I ask You to remind me of that and help me take comfort in Your Word. Help me to fight through the discouragement, disappointment, and setbacks that I face. I know I'm destined to win—if I don't quit. I ask You for the wisdom I need to navigate forward so there is no wasted effort. I ask for the strength to go forward and the precision to obey Your commands promptly and efficiently. Thank You, Father.

In Jesus' name, amen.

Scriptures

"I have told you these things, so that in Me you may have [perfect] peace and confidence. In the world you have tribulation and trials and distress and frustration; but be of good cheer [take courage; be confident, certain, undaunted]! For I have overcome the world. [I have deprived it of power to harm you and have conquered it for you.]"

—JOHN 16:33 (AMP)

Now thanks be unto God, which always causeth us to triumph in Christ, and maketh manifest the savour of his knowledge by us in every place.

—2 CORINTHIANS 2:14 (KJV)

But thanks be to God, Who gives us the victory [making us conquerors] through our Lord Jesus Christ.

—1 CORINTHIANS 15:57 (AMP)

"In conclusion, be strong in the Lord be empowered through your union with Him; draw your strength from Him that strength which His boundless might provides. Put on God's whole armor the armor of a heavy-armed soldier which God supplies, that you may be able successfully to stand up against all the strategies and the deceits of the devil."

—EPHESIANS 6:10-11 (AMPC)

Thoughts

"Success is failure turned inside out— The silver tint of the clouds of doubt; So stick to the fight when you're hardest hit— It's when things seem worst that you must not quit."

—Edgar A. Guest

Thank goodness for all of the things you are not!
Thank goodness you're not
something someone forgot,
and left all alone in some punkerish place
like a rusty tin coat hanger hanging in space.
That's why I say "Duckie!
don't grumble! don't stew!
some critters are much-much,
oh, ever so much-much,
so muchly much-much more unlucky than you!"

—Dr. Seuss

"Gratitude is an offering precious in the sight of God, and it is one that the poorest of us can make and be not poorer but richer for having made it."

—A.W. Tozer

26

Thankfulness

The transformative power of gratitude is a formidable force in the life of a believer. It transcends the ritual of a mealtime prayer or a fleeting acknowledgment when someone extends a kindness. Gratitude is the lens of faith and humility through which all situations, be they favorable or challenging, are viewed. It is an unwavering declaration that in every circumstance, one can find reasons to be thankful. This spirit of gratitude declares that there is no obstacle on Earth insurmountable for those equipped by God. There is no darkness so deep that God's light cannot penetrate. There is no chasm so wide that His love cannot bridge.

To waste the breath God has graciously given us on complaints rather than thanksgiving should be an afront to us. The spirit of gratitude can be boiled down to a simple phrase:

"Appreciate everything, Expect nothing."

This isn't about thanking God for the hardships themselves, as if He orchestrates our pain as lessons. The bible tells us to give thanks "in all things," not to give thanks "For all things." Thanksgiving is about recognizing that we are owed nothing, and thus, everything we have is a gift. The bounty of salvation, grace, and love we receive through Christ is not our due but a generous offering. We are not entitled to life, joy, peace, or freedom; yet, we have access to these blessings through the divine gift of God.

This perspective isn't about passive acceptance but a dynamic, faith-filled shift that reorients our entire being. It's about seeing every moment, every breath, every heartbeat as part of a grander narrative woven by the hands of our loving Father. When we truly embrace this mindset, the mundane becomes miraculous, the ordinary becomes extraordinary, and our daily lives become a canvas for God's grace.

In this light, gratitude becomes our compass, guiding us through life's tumultuous seas and serene harbors alike. It is a powerful alchemy that turns trials into triumphs and despair into hope. It is the acknowledgment that even in our darkest hours, there are glimmers of light to be found - if only we have the eyes to see them.

So let us walk in this attitude of gratitude, knowing that every challenge is an opportunity for growth, every setback a setup for a comeback. Let us remember that our journey is not just about reaching a destination but about appreciating every step along the way. With hearts full of thankfulness, let us look to each new day with anticipation, embracing all that life offers with open arms and a spirit that says, "I am grateful, for I am blessed beyond measure." This life-altering perspective of gratitude does more than bring a smile to our faces; it ignites a fire in our souls, propelling us forward with joy, hope, and an unshakeable faith in the goodness of God.

Prayer

Lord, there is no better time to say "thank You" than the present. I thank You for the opportunity to show gratitude to You each and every day. Thank You, Lord, for saving me, for writing my name in the Lamb's Book of Life. Thank You for adopting me into Your family, for making it possible for me to spend eternity with You in heaven. I also thank You for Your Word, which brings faith, stability, life, joy, peace, and strength into my life. Your Word shows me Your character and Your thoughts toward me. Thank You for Your unconditional love, which has been shed abroad for me. Thank You for never leaving me, nor forsaking me. Thank You for hearing my prayers, for listening to me when I call upon You. Thank You for sending Your Son to die for me. Thank You for this day, which You have made. Thank You for allowing me to learn and grow in my faith, and to seek You each and every day.

Lord, I ask for Your help to maintain an attitude of gratitude, regardless of anything that is going on in my life. Help me to keep my mind fixed on You, and to meditate and think only on what is true, honest, right, clean, and pure—things that are lovely and things that are good. Help me to cultivate a lifestyle of thanksgiving so that I never give in to the feelings of despair and hopelessness, but rather act as a pillar of strength and faith for my family, my friends, and my community. What a joyous journey I have the privilege of undertaking with my family, friends, and You—my God. Help me never to lose sight of that all my days.

In Jesus' name, amen.

Scriptures

Be joyful always; pray continually; give thanks in all circumstances, for this is God's will for you in Christ Jesus.

—1 THESSALONIANS 16-18 (NIV)

And whatever you do, whether in word or deed, do it all in the name of the Lord Jesus, giving thanks to God the Father through him.

—COLOSSIANS 3:17 (NIV)

Be earnest and unwearied and steadfast in your prayer [life], being [both] alert and intent in [your praying] with thanksgiving.

—COLOSSIANS 4:2 (AMP)

Be careful for nothing; but in everything by prayer and supplication with thanksgiving let your requests be made known unto God.

—PHILIPPIANS 4:6 (KJV)

"Enter his gates with thanksgiving and his courts with praise; give thanks to him and praise his name. For the Lord is good and his love endures forever; his faithfulness continues through all generations."

—PSALM 100:4-5 (NIV)

Thoughts

"No matter how choppy the seas become, a believer's heart is buoyed by constant praise and gratefulness to the Lord."

—John MacArthur

"Your time is limited, so don't waste it living someone else's life. Don't be trapped by dogma—which is living with the results of other people's thinking. Don't let the noise of others' opinions drown out your own inner voice. And most important, have the courage to follow your heart and intuition."

—Steve Jobs

"Twenty years from now you will be more disappointed by the things that you didn't do than by the ones you did do. So throw off the bowlines. Sail away from the safe harbor. Catch the trade winds in your sails. Explore. Dream. Discover."

—Mark Twain

27

Feeling Trapped

If you've ever reached a point where you feel like you've exhausted all your options, where giving up seems like the only choice left, then you know what it's like to feel truly trapped. It's a place where change seems impossible, where helplessness and hopelessness are your constant companions, and where you question every aspect of your life, including its very worth. In these moments of despair, life feels like a puzzle with missing pieces, or like being lost in a dense forest without a map. You look around and see others seemingly moving forward effortlessly, while you feel frozen in time, unable to find your way.

You are not alone in your struggle; many have felt trapped by their circumstances. The good news is, there is a way out, even though you can't see it right now. God is the missing puzzle piece. God is your map in the forest. God is your way maker. The only way you are going to make it out of your prison is to let God into it and trust Him to guide you out.

True freedom from challenging situations is rarely an overnight event. It's a gradual process that starts with a grain of hope: admitting to yourself that change is possible and that, with God, you can find joy and light again in your life. It's about believing that no situation is too bleak, no night too dark, and that the dawn will come.

Once you embrace this grain of hope, you have to rid yourself of all the poison inside your heart and mind. We do this by forgiving others and then by taking our problems, emotions, and pain to God. The Bible encourages us to cast all our anxieties on Him because He cares for us. We do this every day, through casting down negative thoughts of hopelessness and complaining. You can control what you think about. It's not enough to get rid of the bad; you have to replace it with the good.

Listening to and reading God's words and promises is essential in this process. The Bible is not just a book; it's a living conversation between God and humanity. Within its pages lie promises of strength, healing, and guidance. Believing these promises means more than just understanding them; it means letting them take root in your heart and transform your perspective. Meditate on these things. Instead of complaining, as an act of faith, lift up your voice and praise God, especially when you don't feel like it.

After going through this daily process for some time, we become more sensitive to the voice of God, which opens the door to His guidance. That is the final step that leads you out of your prison. When God guides you towards a path, no matter how unconventional or challenging it may seem, follow it. This obedience is often where the greatest transformations happen. It might be a call to forgive, to let go of past hurts, or to take a step of faith into a new chapter of your life. Whatever form it takes, this obedience is the key to escaping your prison.

Prayer

Lord, I thank You for making a way where there seems to be no way, when I can see no way out. Thank You for never leaving me alone to deal with the issues of this life, especially when the problems I face are of my own making. Thank You for Your mercy and grace, which are greater than any of my mistakes or weaknesses. Thank You that Your strength and wisdom are greater than the pain and confusion that is before me. Father, I know that according to Your Word, wherever You are, there is freedom. I ask for Your help in fully manifesting that freedom in my life. Help me see this situation as you see it, and help me to know where I can apply my faith to overcome the obstacles, where to trust in You to make a way of an escape. Help me to know when it is time to fight and when it is time to rest. Help me see the light and hope of freedom once again.

Heavenly Father, You know the feelings I feel and how blinding and overwhelming the challenges of this life can seem. These problems definitely not fun — so, Lord, I'm asking You to work a miracle in my life. My first step of faith in this matter is to cast the weight of my responsibilities off my shoulders and onto Yours. I place my pain, my confusion, and my hopelessness at Your feet, and I ask for Your peace and joy to take their place. I ask for wisdom and guidance as I take my next step. Help me to hope again, to live boldly and confidently in remembrance of Your promises toward me, and to be assured beyond any doubt that You will make a way for me. If You require anything from me, Lord, I commit to doing it. Thank You, Lord, for helping me.

In Jesus' name, amen.

Scriptures

"If you'll hold on to me for dear life," says God, "I'll get you out of any trouble. I'll give you the best of care if you'll only get to know and trust me. Call me and I'll answer, be at your side in bad times; I'll rescue you, then throw you a party. I'll give you a long life, give you a long drink of salvation!"

—PSALM 91:14-16 (MSG)

For the Lord is the Spirit, and wherever the Spirit of the Lord is, there is freedom.

—2 CORINTHIANS 3:17 (NLT)

"But I'll take the hand of those who don't know the way, who can't see where they're going. I'll be a personal guide to them, directing them through unknown country. I'll be right there to show them what roads to take, make sure they don't fall into the ditch. These are the things I'll be doing for them—sticking with them, not leaving them for a minute."

—ISAIAH 42:16 (MSG)

"I waited patiently for the LORD; he turned to me and heard my cry. He lifted me out of the slimy pit, out of the mud and mire; he set my feet on a rock and gave me a firm place to stand. He put a new song in my mouth, a hymn of praise to our God."

—PSALM 40:1-3 (NIV)

Thoughts

"When we are no longer able to change a situation, we are challenged to change ourselves."

—VICTOR FRANKL (Holocaust survivor)

"In the same way the sun never grows weary of shining, nor a stream of flowing, it is God's nature to keep His promises. Therefore, go immediately to His throne and say, 'Do as You promised.'"

—CHARLES SPURGEON

"Are you tired? Worn out? Burned out on religion? Come to me. Get away with me and you'll recover your life. I'll show you how to take a real rest. Walk with me and work with me— watch how I do it. Learn the unforced rhythms of grace. I won't lay anything heavy or ill-fitting on you. Keep company with me and you'll learn to live freely and lightly."

—JESUS (Matthew 11:28-30 MSG)

28

Weariness

Weariness is not being tired at the end of the day, nor a lack of energy when starting the day. Weariness is when your soul is bone tired; when your situation feels endless; and your perspective is tainted with hopelessness. Weariness can creep into your life in many different ways. You can become weary from the grind of everyday life, from trying to balance all your responsibilities, from doing the right thing without recognition or reward, from years of unfulfilled potential and dreams, from overcommitting yourself, or from trying to keep up daily appearances.

It's easy to settle for the fake peace the world prescribes, using entertainment, medications, and alcohol to escape the barrage of pressures and responsibilities that assail our lives daily. The problem with this kind of momentary cease fire is we have come back to the same life we tried to forget. Whatever the cause for the weariness in your life, the answer is the same. Jesus said "come to me all who are weary and I will give you rest."

God never meant for us to be dependent on anyone or anything besides Himself. The same peace that Jesus operated in is available for us, to live in a tranquil state, with our soul secured due to our trust in God. If you are not resting on the inside, with a mind quieted by this peace, then you cannot rest on the outside, finding rejuvenation for your body. So carve out time every day to spend with God to enjoy and refresh yourself in His Word. Seek out wisdom for what commitments you need to maintain and which ones you need to let go. Finally, rest in the Lord, casting all the weight of your life and its problems on Him, because you know He'll take care of you.

Life can be a dull struggle for survival, barely staying afloat in the sea of endless responsibilities and expectations, or life can be a glorious adventure that you undertake with your friends, family, and your God.

Don't let weariness rob you of the joys and marvels of this season in your life. This journey, filled with challenges and triumphs, is not about surviving but learning to enjoy the little things. It's like having a newborn; you can become so weary taking care of your child, desperately fantasizing about a time when you'll get a full night's sleep, that you might miss the incredible and special moments you have with your precious little one. Ask for God's help to enjoy this season, whatever that may be, and to notice the beauty in the mundane and the extraordinary in the ordinary.

Each day then becomes an opportunity to make a difference, to touch a life, to learn something new, to share a special moment, and to grow. Choose to see your life as an adventure, and enjoy your voyage.

Prayer

Lord, I thank You for the ability to hope in You. Your Word says that when I wait, expect, look for, and hope in You, then You will renew my strength and power. You will cause me to lift my wings and mount up close to You as an eagle mounts up to the sun. When I wait on You, I shall run and not be weary; I shall walk and not be faint or become tired. Thank You, Father! My soul finds rest in You, and because You keep me safe, I can sleep in peace. Father, You know that it is so easy for Your people to allow fatigue and sheer exhaustion to overshadow the truth of Your Word. It's easy to allow these external problems to turn into internal issues of weariness and depression. So, Lord, I ask for Your help to shore up my defenses against the enemy of weariness in my life.

I ask for wisdom in the practical matters of life in this world. If there are things I am wasting my energy on physically, or thoughts and pressures I'm meditating on mentally that I ought not to focus on, I ask that You would reveal that to me so I can get rid of these things in my life. I ask for You to guide me through Your Word and Your peace. Create space in my days so that I can catch my breath with You and truly rest in Your arms. Help me to keep my focus on You, instead of the trials I go through. Encourage me and comfort me, especially when the grind of life saps my energy. Finally, Lord, I ask that You would help me trust in You during the labor I put forth in Your name, so that I would not grow weary while doing good. Help me to remember the harvest will surely come if I don't lose heart.

Thank You, Lord, for all these things. In Jesus' name, amen.

Scriptures

And let us not grow weary while doing good, for in due season we shall reap if we do not lose heart.

—GALATIANS 6:9 (NKJV)

Truly my soul finds rest in God; my salvation comes from him.

—PSALM 62:1 (NIV)

In peace I will lie down and sleep, for you alone, O Lord, will keep me safe.

—PSALM 4:8 (NLT)

But those who wait for the Lord [who expect, look for, and hope in Him] shall change and renew their strength and power; they shall lift their wings and mount up [close to God] as eagles [mount up to the sun]; they shall run and not be weary, they shall walk and not faint or become tired.

—ISAIAH 40:31 (AMP)

"Therefore, since we are surrounded by such a great cloud of witnesses, let us throw off everything that hinders and the sin that so easily entangles. And let us run with perseverance the race marked out for us, fixing our eyes on Jesus, the pioneer and perfecter of faith. For the joy set before him he endured the cross, scorning its shame, and sat down at the right hand of the throne of God. Consider him who endured such opposition from sinners, so that you will not grow weary and lose heart."

—HEBREWS 12:1-3 (NIV)

Thoughts

"When you arise in the morning, think of what a precious privilege it is to be alive—to breathe, to think, to enjoy, to love."

—MARCUS AURELIUS

"The Christian life is not a constant high. I have my moments of deep discouragement. I have to go to God in prayer with tears in my eyes, and say, 'O God, forgive me,' or 'Help me.'"

—Billy Graham

"Every person who has grown to any degree of usefulness, every person who has grown to distinction, almost without exception has been a person who has risen by overcoming obstacles, by removing difficulties, by resolving that when he met discouragement he would not give up."

—Booker T. Washington

29

Discouragement

Discouragement is a stealthy adversary, often creeping up on us when we least expect it. It's particularly insidious when we're mired in adverse circumstances for a prolonged period. But it's important to realize that this feeling is more than mere disappointment, discontent, or frustration. It's a deeper, more sinister force, akin to a negative spiritual undertow that can strip away our joy and peace.

This sense of discouragement manifests in various forms. It can produce a profound sense of hopelessness, paralyzing our lives and clouding our perspectives. It's like a shadow that dims even the brightest of moments, a subtle pain that can feel almost physical in its intensity. Discouragement saps our strength and confidence, incessantly reminds us of our failures, and blinds us to our blessings. It's a gateway to more profound struggles like depression and insecurity, making mountains out of molehills and magnifying our doubts and fears.

In these moments of vulnerability, we often confront a harsh truth. We recognize our limitations – that we aren't always strong enough, smart enough, or talented enough to achieve what we're meant for. It is in moments like these that we realize that we need something greater than ourselves to reach our full potential. We need God's presence in our lives to fulfill our destiny.

The problem arises when we base our identity, happiness, and strength solely on our achievements or failures. When we do this, we set ourselves up for a fall. We become susceptible to discouragement and hurt, as these things are bound to change. Instead, we must find our foundation in something more steadfast and unchanging. God should be our source of happiness and strength, and it is in Him that we should anchor our self-worth, not in the shifting sands of people's opinions, life's unpredictable circumstances, nor our accomplishments.

To combat discouragement, it's crucial to immerse ourselves in God's Word, to meditate on His promises and to focus on the blessings in our lives rather than the problems. It's about shifting our perspective from the temporal to the eternal, from the worldly to the divine. Let God's love envelop you – through praise, worship, prayer, and reflection on His Word.

To be discouraged is, in many ways, to believe a lie. It's to forget the truths that God has spoken over our lives. When we truly embrace what God's Word says about us, then the strength, once sapped by discouragement, begins to energize our efforts once again. It's from here that we must stay vigilant and develop a resilience against discouragement by constantly spending time with the Lord and reminding ourselves who He says we are and what He says we can do. This will cultivate a mindset that treats every setback, every disappointment, and every failure as reason to dig deeper and deeper into God's word, to reach higher with our praise, and go further with Him in Prayer.

In doing so, we not only overcome discouragement but transform it into a catalyst for developing a deeper, more meaningful relationship with God. Who can defeat somebody like that?

Prayer

Lord, I know that discouragement is not a condition of the body, but a poison that seeps into the soul when I believe a lie and focus on the wrong things. As such, I take this moment to echo the sentiments expressed by Your disciples in the Scriptures, and I declare that I will not allow myself to become discouraged—utterly spiritless, exhausted, and worn out through fear. You have commanded me to be strong and courageous and not to be afraid or discouraged, because You are with me. You are my God, and I am Your child. Any issue that I face, even if it is due to my own shortcoming or inadequacy, Your Word clearly states that You will strengthen me and help me to overcome. You will hold me up, no matter what situation I am facing.

So, Lord, I come to You now to receive the help that You promised. Remove the poison of discouragement from my soul. Encourage me, for Your joy is my strength, Your peace is my guide, and Your presence is my protection. I know that even though my own strength may fail, Your strength will pick up the slack. I know that even when I feel hurt and alone, You are with me, and You stand ready to help me. So I ask for that very thing right now. Remind me that You are near to me; remind me that I'm Yours, and that Your plans for me are greater than any closed door, any heartbreaking situation, or any setback. With You by my side as my Encourager, I know that I will be okay. Thank You, Lord.

In Jesus' name, amen.

Scriptures

Don't be afraid, for I am with you. Don't be discouraged, for I am your God. I will strengthen you and help you. I will hold you up with my victorious right hand.

—Isaiah 41:10 (NLT)

"This is my command—be strong and courageous! Do not be afraid or discouraged. For the Lord your God is with you wherever you go."

—Joshua 1:9 (NLT)

But God, who encourages those who are discouraged, encouraged us by the arrival of Titus.

—2 Corinthians 7:6 (NLT)

Therefore we do not become discouraged (utterly spiritless, exhausted, and wearied out through fear). Though our outer man is [progressively] decaying and wasting away, yet our inner self is being [progressively] renewed day after day.

—2 Corinthians 4:16 (AMP)

"Why, my soul, are you downcast? Why so disturbed within me? Put your hope in God, for I will yet praise him, my Savior and my God."

—Psalm 42:11 (NIV)

Thoughts

I have been given eyes to see and a mind to think, and now I know a great secret of life, for I perceive, at last, that all my problems, discouragements , and heartaches are, in truth, great opportunities in disguise.

—Og Mandino

"Renew, release, let go. Yesterday's gone. There's nothing you can do to bring it back. You can't should've done something. You can only DO something. Renew yourself. Release that attachment. Today is a new day!"

—Steve Maraboli

"You can't go back and change the beginning, but you can start where you are and change the ending."

—CS Lewis

30

The Past

The past is a common thread in all our lives, unchangeable and ever-present. For some, it's a golden era, idealized as life's best chapter. Yet, for others, it's a shadow, laced with regret or relentless fixation. Our past is like a mosaic of moments, choices, and thoughts—some of which bring a flush of embarrassment or a wave of unease at their mere recollection. Haven't we all longed, at times, for the wisdom of now in our yesterdays? And many have weathered storms not of their making: the scars of abuse, the strain of toxic ties, the sting of efforts unseen and unappreciated.

"How different would things be if I knew then what I know now?" We've all pondered this, a seemingly harmless musing. Yet, such reflections can ensnare us, spinning a web of regrets and hypotheticals. It's important to realize that being anchored in bygone days serves no purpose. Learning from the past is crucial, but dwelling there is a road to nowhere. In fact, it can be counterproductive, even damaging. Our journey forward isn't about erasing our history but about embracing the lessons it offers without letting it overshadow our current path. We mustn't let the shadows of yesterday eclipse the brightness of today and the potential of tomorrow. To break free from the shackles of regret and shame, it's essential to refocus and renew our minds. This involves shifting our thoughts from past pains to the positive aspects of our lives.

The Past

Your relationship with God, your connections with friends and family, all exist vibrantly in the present. Your life unfolds in the here and now, not in the echoes of yesterday. It's in the current moment that you can experience the warmth of a friend's smile, the comforting embrace of a family member, or the profound peace found in your heavenly Father. Focus on the joys of today, the laughter shared, the conversations that uplift, and the simple moments of contentment that often go unnoticed. Embrace the spontaneous and the routine alike, finding beauty in the everyday interactions and the quiet reflections. Let these present experiences, rather than the shadows or even the highlights of the past, color your world and shape your perspective.

Don't believe the lie that you have to delve deep into your past to understand who you are and why you do what you do. There is a better way to heal, Its by diving into the word of God. You must replace your thoughts of regret and shame by renewing your mind with What your loving heavenly father has said concerning you. Instead of dwelling on all the hurts and pains of the past, dwell on all the things that God has said about you and done for you.

God doesn't see you in the light of your past, He sees you in the light of His Son's sacrifice! You are in right standing with your Father, God. When He looks at you He sees His beautiful creation, His best friend, His child. You have the love of God to heal your heart from the pain of your past; to place a new identity upon you and a new power within you. Your present situation is changeable, and the future of your dreams attainable! With His love healing your past, His strength reinforcing your present, and the power of His promises guaranteeing your future, you are defined by and destined for greatness.

The Past

Prayer

Thank You, Lord, for Your forgiveness, for Your grace, and for Your mercy. You said in Your Word that You have forgiven and forgotten my sins, that You have cast them from me as far as the east is from the west. I am so thankful that You don't see me in the light of what I have done, but that You look upon me in light of what Jesus has done on the cross. I thank You that I have the right and the privilege to come to You with boldness, especially when I make a mistake, to receive Your help and encouragement. All this is due to the finished work of Jesus. I thank You that my past does not define my future, and that You do not consult my past to determine what kind of life my future will hold. You said in Your Word that when You begin a work in someone's life, You are faithful to see it through to completion. I thank You for sticking with me, for not giving up on me despite everything I have done.

Father, I know You have a plan and a purpose for me. I ask for Your help to govern my perspective—according to Your Word and not according to my past experiences. Help me not to build upon my experience but to build upon Your Word. Help me to lean on You instead of my own understanding. Help me to move on with my life, to leave the past behind me, and to reach toward the future You have planned for me. Help me to forgive myself and let go of my past. Help me to forget the former things and look forward—toward the future. Help me to fulfill the destiny and the plans You have for me. I thank You that You are doing a new thing in my life. I know I cannot go forward by looking backward, and so I commit not to let the mistakes of my past keep me from making good decisions for the future. I make the conscious choice to look forward expectantly to a bright and wonderful future with You.

In Jesus' name, amen.

Scriptures

"Forget the former things; do not dwell on the past. See, I am doing a new thing! Now it springs up; do you not perceive it? I am making a way in the wilderness and streams in the wasteland."

—ISAIAH 43:18-19 (NIV)

Therefore if any man be in Christ, he is a new creature: old things are passed away; behold, all things are become new.

—2 CORINTHIANS 5:17 (KJV)

No, dear brothers and sisters, I have not achieved it, but I focus on this one thing: forgetting the past and looking forward to what lies ahead, I press on to reach the end of the race and receive the heavenly prize for which God, through Christ Jesus, is calling us.

—PHILIPPIANS 3:13-14 (NLT)

"Therefore, since we are surrounded by such a great cloud of witnesses, let us throw off everything that hinders and the sin that so easily entangles. And let us run with perseverance the race marked out for us, fixing our eyes on Jesus, the pioneer and perfecter of faith. For the joy set before him he endured the cross, scorning its shame, and sat down at the right hand of the throne of God."

—HEBREWS 12:1-2 (NIV)

Thoughts

"Never look back unless you are planning to go
that way."

—HENRY DAVID THOREAU

"Everything can be taken from a man but one thing: the last of human freedoms—to choose one's attitude in any given set of circumstances, to choose one's own way."

—Viktor E. Frankl (Holocaust Survivor)

"Happiness is a choice, not a result. Nothing will make you happy until you choose to be happy. No person will make you happy unless you decide to be happy. Your happiness will not come to you. It can only come from you."

—Ralph Marston

31

Making Good Choices

Letting your heart not be troubled is a choice. Keeping calm and trusting God in the midst of every heartache, challenge, setback, failure, and disappointment is a choice. A choice to cast all of your worries, all of your anxiety, and all of your fears onto your Heavenly Father. A choice to seek help for others when they need help. A choice to find good in any situation. A choice to smile without a reason and to love without a cause. A choice to hope in hopeless situations. A choice to trust God in the midst of a treacherous storm, and to rejoice with Him in the midst of the best life has to offer. A choice to surrender control of your life over to your Heavenly Father. A choice to live in the present, to hope in the future and learn from the past. A choice to let God in so He can then get you out. A choice to believe your Father's Word over the world's lies. A choice to remember your blessings instead of your mistakes. A choice to lean on God for strength when you feel you can't take another step. A choice to fill the gaps of your abilities with faith in God's. A choice to fill the hole created by loss with God's love. A choice to be lost in

God's presence instead of an addiction. A choice to give up walking alone and accept the helping hand of your Father. A choice to fight against what is evil, and to love what is good. A choice to believe in God when no one on this earth believes in you, because He believes in you. A choice to think on what is good, and not on what is evil. A choice to live and walk by faith. A Choice to believe the best in everyone while guarding your heart from the worst. A choice to raise your voice for justice and truth, even when every instinct urges you to seek the comfort of silence and safety. A choice to embrace silence and restraint, resisting the urge to retaliate with sharp words, even when others have wounded you with theirs. A choice to smile in faith when you feel like crying in despair.

The truth is God is your daddy, and the greatest gift that He has given you is the ability to choose Him. For it can be your choice, in the midst of the mess this world is in, with so many options for you to choose over Him, to still surrender all that you are, and run into His loving arms and say "I choose you." Choose Him . . . choose to let your heart not be troubled.

Prayer

Lord, I thank You for the power of free will, which You have given to every person. Thank You for creating a place where we have the right of governance to choose in every situation. I know that because of this free will, humanity has made some pretty bad choices, and it is only by Your grace and mercy that we are afforded the opportunity to now make some good choices instead. You said in Your Word that You have set before us life and death—and that Your desire is for us to choose life. I understand that every day has two handles: I can choose to focus on all the problems facing me and choose death, or I can focus on You and choose life instead.

I understand that the collection of my choices are the building blocks of my life and of my future. As such, I ask for Your supernatural help to make the right choices. I ask for Your guidance and direction for the choices that I make. Help me to discern Your will and to hear Your voice. I ask for Your divine wisdom in all my affairs. Help me not to be overly influenced in my decision-making by my emotions, nor to be swayed by the opinions of others. Help me to slow down and relax when I feel pressured, so that I can make the right choice.

When I'm tempted to let my situation dictate the type of day I am having, the thoughts I'm thinking, or the feelings I'm experiencing, I ask for You to remind me that my attitude is a choice—and not the result of what is happening around me. Remind me to put more value on Your words than on the words or advice of anyone else. Help me to place more value on Your will for my life than for my own will or others' desires for my life. Help me not to make rushed choices, but to prayerfully consider all options before making a major decision. Help me in my mission to live a life of service to You, and to seek Your Kingdom first.

In Jesus' name, amen.

Scriptures

"Today I have given you the choice between life and death, between blessings and curses. Now I call on heaven and earth to witness the choice you make. Oh, that you would choose life, so that you and your descendants might live!"

—DEUTERONOMY 30:19 (NLT)

My counsel is this: Live freely, animated and motivated by God's Spirit. Then you won't feed the compulsions of selfishness. For there is a root of sinful self-interest in us that is at odds with a free spirit, just as the free spirit is incompatible with selfishness. These two ways of life are antithetical, so that you cannot live at times one way and at times another way according to how you feel on any given day. Why don't you choose to be led by the Spirit and so escape the erratic compulsions of a law-dominated existence?

—GALATIANS 5:16-18 (MSG)

"You, my brothers and sisters, were called to be free. But do not use your freedom to indulge the flesh; rather, serve one another humbly in love."

—GALATIANS 5:13 (NIV)

"Here I am! I stand at the door and knock. If anyone hears my voice and opens the door, I will come in and eat with that person, and they with me."

—REVELATION 3:20 (NIV)

Thoughts

"Choices are the hinges of destiny."

—Edwin Markham

Keep Calm & Trust God Vol 1
Issues such as anxiety, worry, fear, stress, setbacks, failures, etc. are addressed. Includes prayers, short narratives, scripture, poems and encouraging short stories – all directed to how to keep your cool and trust God.
$4.99

Keep Calm & Trust God Vol 2
Following in the footsteps of the bestseller Keep Calm and Trust God, volume 2 provides even more encouragement in love, hope, peace, joy, courage and faith. Includes prayers, short narratives, scripture poems and encouraging short stories.
$4.99

Keep Calm & Trust God Gift Edition
Bestsellers *Keep Calm and Trust God* and *Keep Calm and Trust God, Volume 2* are now combined together in a beautiful hardcover gift edition. It is arranged by topic to offer short stories, prayers, scripture and poems on whatever situation you may be facing. With an attractive cover, this edition is a welcome gift for friends and family.
$12.99

Let Not Your Heart Be Troubled
Written to offer hope, encouragement and strength to a world that is under constant assault mentally, emotionally and physically. It is formatted topically to deal with issues such as loss, discouragement, and weariness. Scriptures, quotes, meditations and prayers are included to give answers to impossible questions of life and challenges that lie ahead.
$4.99

Scriptural Prayers for Victorious Living
This bountiful treasury of scripture based on prayer is a powerful tool designed to inspire and equip believers with the confidence needed to pray effectively and efficiently. It provides just the right words to pray scripture and stand on God's promises when faced with crisis, discouragement, fear, rejection, stress and anxiety.
$4.99

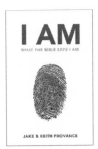

I AM What The Bible Says I AM
Presents seventeen chapters written to clearly reveal the truth of who we are. Each chapter is followed by scripture to take us to the Word and see what God has to say. Words of truth are included to reinforce the truth by speaking it. The perfect tool to discover the reality of who we are in Christ and walk in the fullness of the inheritance He has provided for us.
$4.99

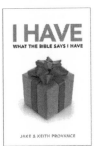

I HAVE What The Bible Says I Have
Written to help new believers, and those who have been God's kids for a while, see the gifts and promises in God's Word and seeks to empower them to live the life God destined them to live. Clearly reveals the truth of what we have in Christ with scripture, and words of truth that can reinforce the truth by speaking it.
$4.99

I Can Do What The Bible Says I Can Do
Designed to offer inspiration and encouragement based on the truths in God's Word and the application of those truths into your life. Believers will be encouraged to overcome any challenge and enjoy victory in every area of life.
$4.99

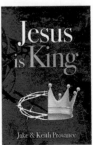

Jesus is King
Written to inspire and encourage us to live in the fullness of life that Jesus Christ provided for us. Every chapter brings understanding and clarity of who Jesus was, what Jesus did, and what He is still doing today! Provides a unique perspective by blending short narratives, scripture and inspired insights by Christian leaders. An extraordinary look at Jesus that will leave a powerful imprint.
$4.99

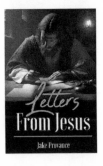

Letters from Jesus
Uniquely weaves a rich tapestry of Scriptures on various topics into heartfelt letters written from the perspective of Jesus. Each letter is crafted with reverence and honor, representing Christ's voice in a personal manner deeply rooted in Scripture. It offers spiritual insight and practical guidance, covering a range of life topics believers encounter.
$14.99

Don't Give Up
All of us, at some point in our lives, will be faced with the choice to press on or to give up. It's in these moments where many are tempted to give up on a relationship, give up on a dream, give up on themselves, or even give up on God. This book is written to interject hope when things look the bleakest, to infuse faith when fear threatens to immobilize, and to remind you of God's love and forgiveness when your heart is heavy. Don't Give Up! God has not given up on you!
$4.99

Burn the Ships
In life, we often find ourselves loaded with excuses that justify why we haven't achieved our goals and realized our dreams. We blame circumstances, others, and sometimes even ourselves or our fate. These excuses act like ships that hover near the shore, always ready to whisk us back to the safety of the known and comfortable whenever challenges arise. It is time to Burn The Ships and live "The No Retreat Life." "The No Retreat Life" champions a lifestyle steeped in steadfast faith and tenacity, where setbacks, remorse, and defeats no longer wear away at your soul but become nourishment for an undaunted spirit.
$4.99

We'd love for you to connect with us at JakeandKeith.com!

Visit us to share your stories, request prayer, and receive a free eBook just for stopping by. Don't forget to scan the QR code below to access our site directly.

Scan Here!